Helena Spyropoulou

EUBOEA

Land of Tradition and History

& SKYROS

EDITIONS
TOUBI'S
ΕΚΔΟΣΕΙΣ
ATHENS 2005

© Copyright 2005   MICHALIS TOUBIS EDITIONS S.A.
Nisiza Karela, Koropi, Attiki
Telephone: +30 210 6029974
Fax: +30 210 6646856
Web Site: http://www.toubis.gr

ISBN: 960-540-608-X

CONTENTS

CONTENTS

1

EUBOEA

LAND OF TRADITION AND HISTORY

The island of Euripus, Euboea, is the ideal destination for a relaxing weekend getaway from the big cities. The reason it is ideal, is because of the close proximity to Athens and the easy access to Attica and the whole of the Central Greece. Euboea is worth a lot more than a weekend trip, though, in order to appreciate all that it has to offer. The island is full of nature's gifts: the soil is rich and fertile, the vegetation is lavish and the coastline is enchanting. The landscape is so full of contrasts, with the mountain villages, the cosmopolitan beaches and the steep and precipitous east coast, that it keeps the visitors' interest on peak. There is wildlife to be enjoyed, mineral springs with therapeutic properties and plenty of contemporary hotels that offer all kinds of modern amenities.

Euboea has a long and tempestuous history, as its archaeological monuments, its Frankish castles and its countless Byzantine churches indicate. The island has been inhabited since the Paleolithic Age and it played a rather important role in the Classical era, but also during the National War of Independence. It is the birthplace of great warriors, artists and scientists. The locals are friendly and welcoming and tradition is always present in every aspect of their lives, their architecture, their language and folklore.

Below: The picturesque village of Steni.
Opposite page: Map of Euboea, chalcography
by G. F. Camocio, 1517-1575.

C.º delle colone.

C.º matello.

Castri

NE

China

Caristo

Paphet
P. raphta

Spuilo.

Arnum

GRO

Caualeni

ACHAIE.

Athica.

Atheue.

Lastura

Marasona

Diro.

Potiri

Caloiero.

Selina

Cupa.

Proismo.

Cardi

PONTE.

Longan.

Mandugo

Vata.

Megra

Valoni.

PARS.

Manclugo.

Lanto.

Badia.

Negro

PONTE.

Trocco

ISO

Ismeno f.

Politica.

Limne.

Talinai.

NEGROPONTE
Infula

Lioso.

Oreo.

LA. Ponico.

Beotia.

Pondico

PROAEMIKON   MONTEION

230

Litan.

N.
Parnai.

Cancua.

C. dfo del vollo.

Ialita.

r. 9

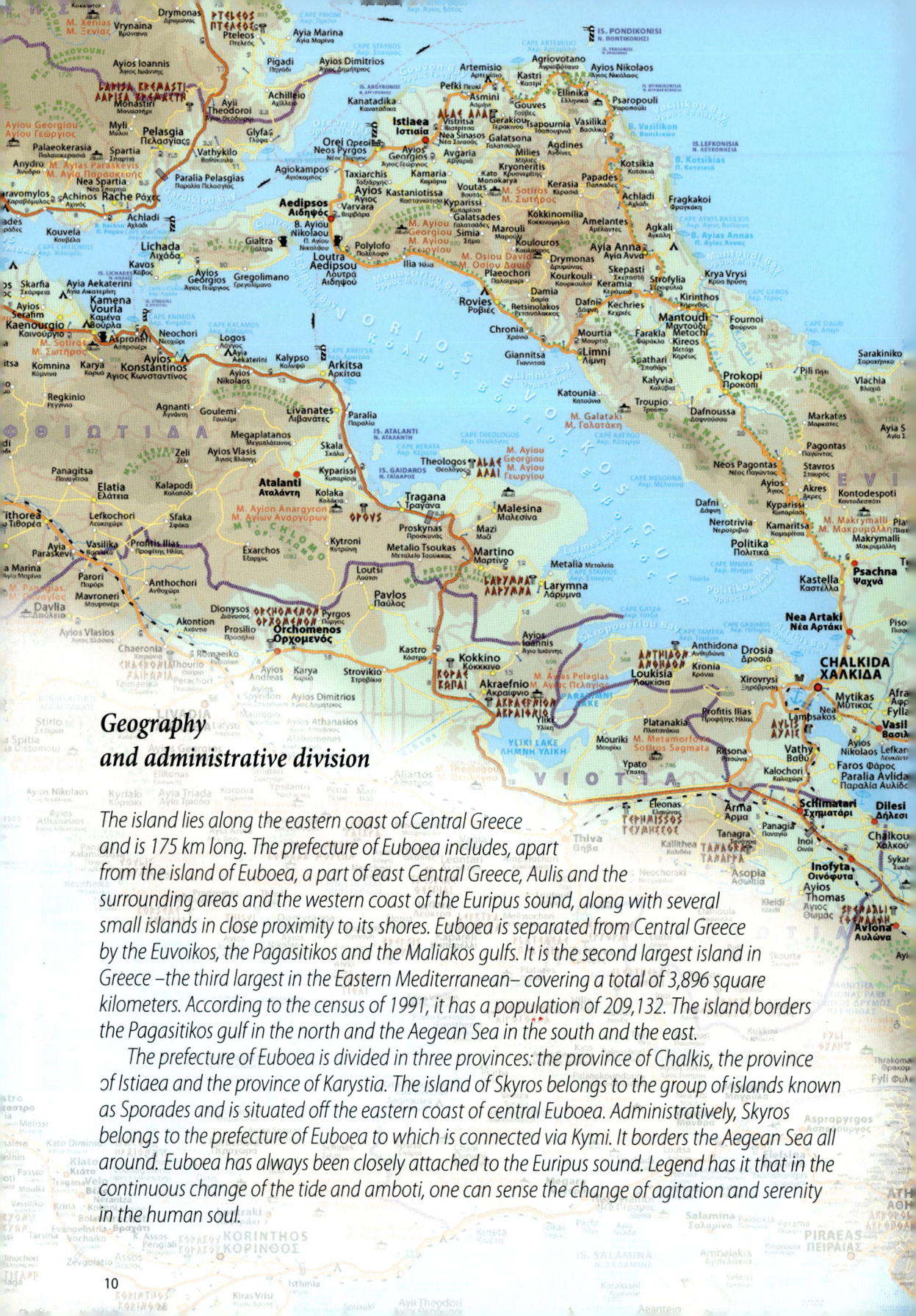

Geography
and administrative division

The island lies along the eastern coast of Central Greece and is 175 km long. The prefecture of Euboea includes, apart from the island of Euboea, a part of east Central Greece, Aulis and the surrounding areas and the western coast of the Euripus sound, along with several small islands in close proximity to its shores. Euboea is separated from Central Greece by the Euvoikos, the Pagasitikos and the Maliakos gulfs. It is the second largest island in Greece –the third largest in the Eastern Mediterranean– covering a total of 3,896 square kilometers. According to the census of 1991, it has a population of 209,132. The island borders the Pagasitikos gulf in the north and the Aegean Sea in the south and the east.

The prefecture of Euboea is divided in three provinces: the province of Chalkis, the province of Istiaea and the province of Karystia. The island of Skyros belongs to the group of islands known as Sporades and is situated off the eastern coast of central Euboea. Administratively, Skyros belongs to the prefecture of Euboea to which is connected via Kymi. It borders the Aegean Sea all around. Euboea has always been closely attached to the Euripus sound. Legend has it that in the continuous change of the tide and amboti, one can sense the change of agitation and serenity in the human soul.

EVIA

IS. SKYROS
Ν. ΣΚΥΡΟΣ

IS. VORIO PODI
Ν. ΒΟΡΕΙΟ ΠΟΔΙ

IS. NOTIO PODI
Ν. ΝΟΤΙΟ ΠΟΔΙ

CAPE KARTSINO
ΑΚΡ. ΚΑΡΤΣΙΝΟ

Trachy
Τραχύ

Katounes
Κατούνες

CAPE POURIA
ΑΚΡ. ΠΟΥΡΙΑ

Atsitsa
Ατσίτσα

Mela
Μελά

Magazia Μαγαζιά

Kyra Panagia
Κυρά Παναγιά

Skyros
Σκύρος

Aspous
Ασπούς

Acherountes
Αχερούντες

Loutro
Λουτρό

MT. KOHYLAS
793

CAPE BORARIA
ΑΚΡ. ΚΟΡΑΚΙΑ

IS. KOULOURI
Ν. ΚΟΥΛΟΥΡΙ

Linaria
Λιναριά

CAPE LIHARI

IS. SKYROPOULA
Ν. ΣΚΥΡΟΠΟΥΛΑ

Skyropoula
Σκυροπούλα

IS. ERINIA
Ν. ΕΡΗΝΙΑ

IS. VALAXA
Ν. ΒΑΛΑΞΑ

CAPE MARMARA
ΑΚΡ. ΜΑΡΜΑΡΑ

Sarakino
Σαρακηνό

IS. SARAKINO
Ν. ΣΑΡΑΚΗΝΟ

IS. EVIA
Ν. ΕΥΒΟΙΑ

ΕΥΒΟΙΑ

OLYMPOS

Legend

—	National road
—	Main asphalt road
—	Asphalt road
—	Non – asphalt road
⛴	Passenger boat route
‖‖‖	Boundaries of Departments
⌷	Archaeological site
▭	Railway
✛	Toll gates
+ 2140	Crests
⌂	Shelter
🎿	Ski run
⚱	Medicinal springs
🏰	Castle
⛽	Gas station
⛪	Monastery
⛺	Camping
◭	Cave
Beach	Beach
⚓	Anchorage
🗼	Lighthouse
🔴	City
🔴	Town
🟡	Village
⚪	Village with 1,000 habitants or more
🟢 STENI	Areas of Outstanding Natural Beauty (AOBN)

Kymi
Κύμη

Aliveri
Αλιβέρι

Karystos
Κάρυστος

Marmari
Μαρμάρι

Nea Makri
Νέα Μάκρη

Rafina
Ραφήνα

Marathonas
Μαραθώνας

Artemis (Loutsa)
Άρτεμις (Λούτσα)

Spata
Σπάτα

Paeania
Παιανία

Markopoulo
Μαρκόπουλο

AIRPORT
ELEFTHERIOS VENIZELOS

SOUTHERN EVOIKOS GULF

PETALION GULF

IS. MEGALONISOS
Ν. ΜΕΓΑΛΟΝΗΣΟΣ

11

Geology

Euboea is mountainous: in the heart of the island we find the ranges of Dirphys (1,743m altitude) and Olympus (1,171m) while in the north, there is the small plain of Istiaea. In the south, in the hinterland of Karystos, there is Ochi, a mountain with an altitude of 1,938 metres. The geologic consistency of Mt Dirphys is predominantly formed of limestone and, while there is hardly any vegetation near the top, as we approach the foot of the mountain, it is covered with dense forests. Mt Ochi dominates the whole area around Karystos, all the way to the Cape Kavodoro. The famous slab-stones of Karystos with the typical grey colour are mined from its sides.

Another ore, vital for the island's economy, is the lignite, which is mainly mined from the area of Aliveri. This lignite falls under the category of xyloid carbon and is formed from the coniferous vegetation of the area. The methodic exploitation of the lignite began in the 20th century, when the "Anonymous Corporation of Aliveri Coal Mines" was founded. In 1951 it was overtaken by the Greek electricity organization.

Morphology

Euboea has a geographic peculiarity: in spite of it being, technically, an island, it is considered as an extension of the mainland, due to the short distance between them and the easy access through motorways. There is actually a theory that suggests that the island was, at some point, linked to the mainland, and was separated from it when the level of the sea rose, forming the Euvoikos gulf. There are two bridges that cross the channel connecting Euboea with Central Greece. One of them is float and crosses the narrow part of the channel, the Euripus sound. From this bridge, which is a work of science and technology, one can admire the amazing work of nature, the tide. The second bridge is a suspension one, which is situated further south the Euvoikos gulf, in Aulis, and constituted, at the time it was built, a very important achievement of engineering. The west coast of the island is smooth and suitable for construction, that's why most settlements are situated there, rather than along the steep, rocky east coast. The legendary, always tempestuous Cape Kafireas (else known as Kavodoro) is characteristic of this part of the island.

Climate

The climate of Euboea is condinental with mild temperatures close to the sea level, while on higher altitudes, the rain is a lot more frequent and there are lower temperatures. The picture changes above the 1,000 metres. This is the mountainous zone of the coniferous plantation, with dense tall forests of firs, pines and chestnut trees.

1. The medicinal springs in Eretria.
2. The snowy top of Dirphys.
3. Panoramic view of the Ochi mountain.

Flora and fauna

There are all sorts of wild plants and plenty of flowers on the mountains of Euboea: poppies, anemones, anthemides cyclamens and lots more. As we climb higher up towards the summits, we can find some rare endemic species, like the Goulimi's Bell, in the area of Prokopi. Not so high, on the slopes of Mt Dirphys, there are pines, firs and chestnut-trees. Mt Kandeely, in the north of Euboea, is covered with coniferous woods (Pinus halepensis, Pinus nigra, Abies cephalonica). The lower parts of Mt Ochi are covered with plane trees (Platanus orientalis), frygana and sklirofyllous bushes (mainly Quercus coccifera). There is a notable chestnut-tree forest near the highest peak as well as a couple of small rivers, where the Vinus agnus-castus and Nerium oleander can be found.

The island is also rich in wildlife, due to its lush plantations, densely forested mountains and rich soil. The etymology of the word 'Eupnoea' indicates a highly developed cattle-raising industry for which it is renowned. In Chalkis area there has been a great development of poultry farming, as well as poultry trade. The mountains of Euboea are busting with wild rabbits, jackals, squirrels and foxes, while at the reserves we find almost every species of duck there is. The species that breed on the island include the stork Ciconia ciconia (it nests in two separate areas) and the Nanoglarono Sterna albifrons.

Mt Kandeely is a nesting place for birds of prey with many species also breeding in the area, like Pernis apivorus, Aquilla chrysaetos, Hieraaetus fasciatus and possibly Accipiter brevipes, while during the summer months, we can find Falco eleonorae. The island is also important for all the migratory species that pass through, like herons, Plegadis falcinellus and Platalea leukorodia.

1a,β. Nerium oleander. 2. Alkanna graeca.
3. Nature in Euboea.
4. The eagle Aquilla chrysaetos.
5. The stork Ciconia ciconia.
6. The lake Dystos, one of the most important reserves of the island.

2
MYTH AND HISTORY

Silver Aeginetan stater, with
a representation of nymph Euboea
on the obverse.

Mythology

According to the myth, Euboea was created by Poseidon, when, after a conflict with Zeus, he bashed his trident against the land of Lyctonia which broke into three pieces: Euboea, Sardinia and Cyprus.

The myth continues that Hera, Zeus's wife, grew up in Euboea, where he seduced her in the form of a cuckoo. According to Pausanias, Zeus abducted young Hera and took her from Euboea, where she had been brought up by her nurse Makris, to a cave high on Mount Kithaeronas, where they consummated. Very quickly, Hera was fed up with her husband's infidelity, so she left him and went back to Euboea.

Zeus fashioned a wooden model of a young woman, he covered it in a veil, put it on a carriage pulled by oxen and ordered them to wander all around Viotia spreading the rumour that this was his new wife.

When Hera found out, she was furious. She located the carriage and ripped the veil off the model, eager to face her rival. When she realized it was only a dummy, she laughed with her husband's deeds and forgave him.

The island of Skyros is also known from Mythology as the place where Thetis sent her son Achilles to prevent him from taking part in the Trojan War, since the oracle predicted that this would lead to his death. Achilles was brought up in the court of Lycomedes, disguised as a girl and eventually had a son named Neoptolemos, by Dieamea, one of the king's daughters. Odysseus, however, managed to change Thetis' mind with his clever trick, so in the end Achilles led the Greeks against Troy. Odysseus came back to Skyros after Achilles' death, this time in order to realize an oracle given by Elenus, suggesting that Troy would only be defeated if Achilles' son fought beneath its walls.

The renowned king of Athens, Theseas, is said to have died in Skyros, when king Lycomedes pushed him off a cliff and into the sea, because he was afraid he would lose his throne to Theseas.

The sacred healing springs of Aedipsos are also mentioned in Greek mythology, as the place where Hercules used to bathe to recover his strength.

Fresco depicting the disclosure of Achilles by Odysseus, in the palace of king Lycomedes.
From the House of Dioskouroi (3rd cent. B.C., Neapoli, National Museum).

Euboea in Prehistoric and early historic times

The oldest evidence of human presence in Euboea dates from the Palaeolithic era. It consists of tools made of flintstone that were discovered in the midlands, near Nea Artaki, and are believed to have been made in two local workshops. Apparently, during the Neolithic period, the population in the area increased and some settlements were built.

1. Early-Helladic jug, from the location of Manika, near the town of Chalkis (1st half of 15th century B.C., Archaeological Museum of Chalkis).
2. Three-handled, straight-sided Mycenaean alabastron from Lefkandi. The shoulder and body are covered with the figures of a griffin, a roe and a deer. The decoration is in matt white paint on a dark surface (12th century B.C., Archaeological Museum of Eretria).

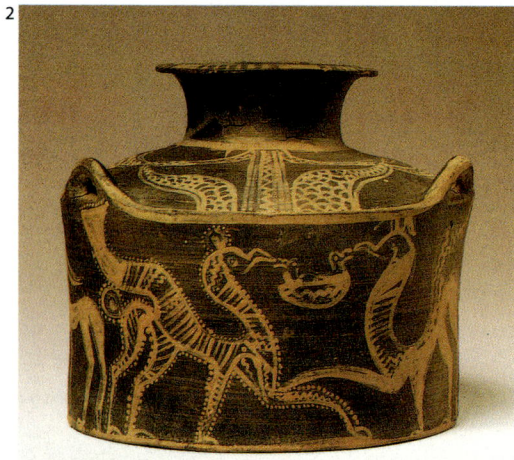

There is strong evidence of human presence on the island of Skyros around this time, too, the most important ones being various objects made of clay.

In the transitional period to the Bronze Age, (3rd millennium B.C.) there are signs of intense commercial activity and contacts with the Kyklades island group, Central Greece and the Asia Minor coast. This is a time of great prosperity for Euboea, which was, apparently, a crossroads between the North and the South Aegean Sea. During this period, a very important part of this activity developed in the area of Manika, in Chalkis, where a whole township of the Early Hellenic period was discovered. In Lefkadi, near Vasiliko, a Mycaenean settlement was found, along with many important objects of the Early Hellenic era, while there are settlements of the same period in Istiaea, Kyrinthos, Psachna, Amarynthos, Artaki, Karystos and Skyros. There are substantial findings of the Mid-Hellenic period in Oraei and Aliveri. Finally, in the vicinity of Chalkis, there have been found interesting tombs of the Post-Hellenic era, while Mycaenean settlements have been discovered in numerous locations.

During the 11th century, some racial mix seems to have taken place in Euboea, as the aeolean tribe of Avandes spread all over the island. The centuries that followed (10th-8th c.), are considered by some historians as the Dark Age for the Hellenic civilization, due to re-enlistment and transfer of the population, although Euboea didn't seem to have been affected, as the important findings of the same period discovered in Lefkadi suggest. These comprise mainly of a hero's monument which was excavated in Ksiropoli, filled with precious gold, ivory and bronze objects, solid evidence of the trading activities between Euboea and Asia Minor, Cyprus and the Aegean islands.

Euboea in Antiquity

Silver Euboean tetradrachm (ca. 500 B.C., Numismatic Museum of Athens).

The first ever collective action in the history of Greece, the Trojan War, started off in Euvoikos bay, where the Greek fleet gathered. Among them, the Euboean tribe, the Avandes, who contributed forty ships to the expeditionary force. In the list of the ships that took part in the war, Homer mentions the Euboean cities Chalkis, Eretria, Istiaea, Kyrinthos, Dion, Karystos and Stira.

In the 7th century, the greek civilization entered a new thriving period and the great age of colonization began. It seems quite possible that the Ionian race that flowed into Euboea, forced the Avandes to Chalkidiki, Chios island and Ionia in Asia Minor. During the second period of colonization, though, the two powerful Euboean cities Eretria and Chalkis, showed a great deal of colonizing activity, establishing colonies in South Italy and Sicily as well as in several other locations along the coast of the Mediterranean Sea and the Euxeinos Pondos. The rivalry between these two cities, that gained wealth and power from their colonies and their navy, led to a lengthy civil war, known as the "Lelandean War" which involved several other Greek cities, allies of the two protagonists.

The other major cities of Euboea (Istiaea, Karystos, Dystos and Kymi) started to flourish during the 6th century as numerous findings of that period, such as coins, suggest. By the end of the century, all the cities had known almost every possible political system -monarchy, aristocracy, oligarchy and tyranny. Later on, the Athenians' expansionism defeated Chalkis and, as a result, Athenian citizens took possession of the land that once belonged to the "hippovotes" –that is the rich Chalkideans– in the Lelandean Plains. This practice was repeated a century later in the vicinity of Istiaea, in the north of the island.

In 499 B.C., the citizens of Eretria joined forces with the Athenian navy and helped the Ionian cities in their revolution against the Persians. It was this that gave the Persians a reason to organize their first expedition against the Greeks during which, they completely destroyed Eretria in reprisal. Another reason why Euboea is associated with the wars between the Greeks and the Persians is because of the sea-fight that took place in Artemision. There, in the northernmost part of the island, the Greek fleet, which included several Euboean ships and crews, collided with the Persians and although the outcome of the conflict was undecided, the Battle of Aremision was a "dress rehearsal" for the naval battle of Salamis. Therefore, the foundations for the freedom of the Greek nation were laid in Artemision, as quoted by the great poet Pindarus.

After the war had ended, many Greek cities joined the First Athenian Alliance, including most of Euboea. The city of Karystos, which at first refused to go down that road, was forced to do so, after having endured several months of siege. When the Athenian Alliance turned into hegemony, the Euboean cities defected twice. The first time, in 446 B.C., Athens reacted very decisively; the Athenian army, led by Pericles himself, attacked Euboea, conquered its cities and restored the Alliance. The second time, though, (441 B.C.), during the Peloponnesian War, the defection of the Euboeans was supported by Peloponnesian forces and Athens lost an important battle in Eretria.

The Euboeans fought alongside the Athenians and the Thebans in the Battle of Chaeronia. After his victory, Phillip most probably mounted guard in Chalkis, since Euboea was considered to be in a very strategic position as far as the control of the southern Greece was concerned. After the Macedonians had taken over Greece, Euboea shared, more or less, the fate of the rest of the Greek cities, with Eretria playing an important role, as the Macedonian tombs that were found at the city cemetery suggest.

1,4. Funerary steles of the Hellenistic period
(Archaeological Museum of Eretria).
2. Macedonian tomb of the 4th century B.C. in Eretria.
3. Part of a statue of Athena, from the temple of Apollo
in Eretria (ca. 500 B.C., Archaeological Museum of Chalkis).
5. View of the archaeological site of Aulis, with the sanctuary
of Aulidean Artemis.

3

4

5

Euboea during the Roman and Byzantine eras and the Latin occupation period

The Romans made the most of the natural assets of Euboea, especially the limestone of Karystos and the mineral springs of Aedipsos. Under the rule of Rome, Chalkis evolved in the trading and cultural centre of the island as suggested by the baths, the archways and the buildings of the city market. It eventually fell into decline, however, and was transferred further to the west, where it stands today.

During the reign of the Byzantines, Euboea fell under the "Greek Issue". Emperor Justinianus fortified the city of Chalkis against barbaric invaders. Evidently, Euboea was a Byzantine province of great importance, as proved by the big number of churches and convents in the vicinity of Chalkis and elsewhere on the island.

After the fall of Constantinople (1204 A.D.) under the Franks, Bonifatios Monferatikos conquered Euboea, which, probably at that point, was renamed Negroponte, due to a mistake in the etymology of the Greek word for Euripus. The island was then divided into three feudal estates and thus the Frankish occupation was firmly established in Euboea. The numerous cubical defense towers scattered all around the island are dated back to this period. During the Venetian rule, the "Kingdom of Negroponte" was a very important commercial centre, efficiently organized in order to facilitate the trade transactions between the Central and Southern Greece.

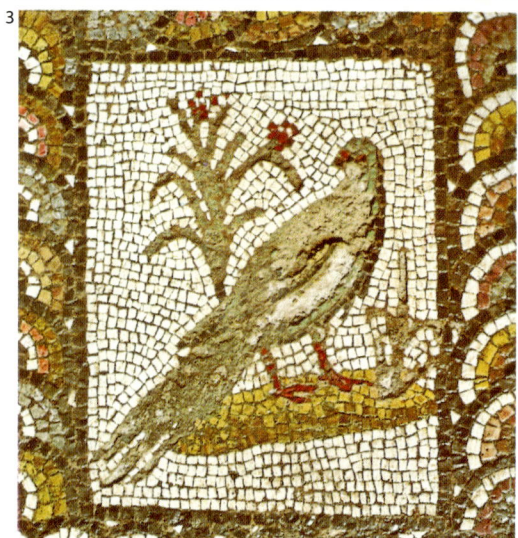

1. Church in the village Politika.
2. Part of the Roman aqueduct in the Kamares area, Chalkis.
3. Roman mosaic floor from the town of Chalkis.
4. Interior view of the church of Ayios Ioannis Rossos.

Euboea under the Turkish rule and the War of Independence of 1821

During the first war between the Turks and the Venetians, Chalkis went under siege and finally fell into the hands of the Turks (1470 A.D.). Following its fall, Euboea along with the North Sporades, which were conquered some time later, constituted the Turkish "pashalik of Egripoz". After a long period under Turkish occupation, the strategic locality of the island arose interest on the part of the Venetians. Morozini, doge of Venice, campaigned against Euboea, with some help from the Greek voluntary army, in 1688, but he failed to conquer the efficiently fortified city of Chalkis, despite a three month long siege. Consequently, Euboea remained under Turkish rule and, together with the east side of Central Greece, comprised a separate administrative region known as the "Sanjak of Euripus" (province). This "sanjak" fell under the bigger administrative division of the White Sea (Aegean Sea) Islands.

The Greek Revolution of 1821 was bound to encounter great difficulties because, due to its strategic position, the Turks had converted it into an unconquerable fortress, with two forts right by the Euripus sound, one in Chalkis and the other across the channel, in Karababa. The first town to rebel against the Turks was Xirochori and Limni, and Kymi followed shortly after Aggelis Govginas or "Govgios" organized the first rebels' camp on Vrysakia location. It was there, where the first big battle took place, when the Turkish army led by Omer Vryonis was defeated and Nickos Krieziotis rose to prominence due to his bravery. However, the Greeks were defeated in another significant battle, the battle of Styra and Petrobey Mavromichalis's son was killed. Following a number of victories over Omer Bey in Diakofti and Vateesi, Krieziotis besieged the town of Karystos, but the Greeks broke camp after the were attacked by the Turkish fleet and the civilians were slaughtered. Krieziotis fled for rescue to Skopelos Island.

When Odysseus Androutsos, as provisional leader, with the help of Psarean ships, laid a siege to the stronghold of Chalkis, Krieziotis returned to Karystos and laid a new siege. Despite the fact that both these investments were well organized and methodical and lasted six months, there just wasn't enough support from the rest of the Greek forces. Consequently, when the Turkish fleet arrived at the Euvoikos Gulf and landed troops on the island, the Greeks had to lift the siege to both cities. Following the end of the siege, the Turks attacked with extreme ferociousness and Euboea went back under the yoke of slavery and suffered the most brutal tyranny. To make things worse, the local warlords' idleness and disputes left little if any room for improvement.

1,2. Portraits of the Euboean soldiers Nikolaos Krieziotis and Aggelis Govginas, who took part in the Greek War of Independence of 1821 (Athens, National Historical Museum).
3. Engraving depicting the Castle of Chalkis, during the period of Turkish domination.

Euboea in recent years

Euboea remained under Turkish rule long after the arrival of Kapodestrias and it wasn't until the 13th of June 1830 that it was finally liberated and incorporated in the young Greek state. It was recognized as a separate prefecture with G. Aenean serving as its first Prefect. He immediately founded a school in Chalkis, which based its operation on the mutual teaching system and also the first printing house. The first newspaper of Euboea, titled "HELLIN", went into circulation a few months later.

For many years after it was liberated, Chalkis maintained its oriental character. In 1885 though, when Charilaos Trikoupis was Prime Minister and Her.Gazepis was the Mayor, the walls of the city were demolished and the debris was used to cover the surrounding moat.

During the Balkan war, Euboea played an important role mainly due to the action of the regiment of the regular army of Chalkis. Renowned for his triumph in the battle of Bizani, is Major Velissarios. Some time later, the Division of Chalkis landed at the coast of liberated Smyrni, in order to take part in the Asia Minor campaign. After the Asia Minor Holocaust in 1922, many refugees arrived in Euboea, the majority of whom settled down in Nea Artaki and Nea Lampsakos as well as in settlements in Chalkis and Amarynthos.

During the Second World War, the Germans bombed Euboea. In April of 1941, German troops entered Chalkis and the "Red House" was used as the command post. At the time of the German occupation, the presence of the Greek resistance was quite conspicuous in Euboea, especially in Lambousa, Steni and Vatonda. The infamous for its brutality civil war that followed, affected the whole island and came to prove, once more, that the civil conflicts can be at least as bad as a national war.

After the liberation of Greece, Euboea made great strides –and continues to do so– as far as its economy and culture are concerned.

1. The "red house" in Chalkis, built in 1884 by the French
   architect Flegise.
2. The National Resistance Memorial in Chalkis.
3. Statue of the Balkan War hero Ioannis Velissarios in Kymi.
4. "Registered trademark" of Chalkis, the Euripus' bridge
   connects Euboea with continental Greece
   (lithography, The Gennadius Library, Athens).

CULTURE AND TRADITION

Folkways

Up until recently, the big events were celebrated in the traditional way in almost every town and village on the island.

Today this is not as common any more, although a number of such customs survive in a few areas of Euboea. There is, for example, the custom of "Kledonas", which takes place on the day of Saint John (24th of June).

The young women of the community gather in one house and, at dusk, a couple of them head to the local public tap to get the "silent water". They, then have to take it to the house without speaking a single word or even smile. If they do, they have to return and get some more water.

Once they've arrived home, all the girls will drop a small object into the container, the so-called "biniotaki" and leave it outside all night, so that it can be seen by the "dawn star". In the morning, the celebrations begin and at noon, the "Kledonas" is opened.

Another tradition is the so-called "piperia"

Costume from Kymi, Euboea.

(pepper) that takes place on the 1st of May in some villages mainly in Northern Euboea and which is basically an allegoric invocation to all the powers of the rain.

The young people of the village gather at the church singing. They "dress" a man in branches and crown him with a wreath of flowers. Then, they wander about the village singing and dancing around this man, the "piperia".

Another young man called "Piperos" hoes people's gardens and the lady of the house sprinkles the ground with water. Altogether they sing the song of "piperia":

Pepper and sweet pomegranate,
Hurry, hurry to Saint Elias
And Saint Elias will hurry to heaven
So that god will let the rain fall.

The women give the children treats, with which they produce meals they enjoy all together, celebrating till night comes.

Another tradition, cheery and spectacular, is the annual revival of the traditional wedding that takes place on Clean Monday, In Ayia Anna.

A great custom that denotes gynaecocracy takes place in the village Vitalo, near Kymi, during the pre-Lenten season ("Apokries"). For the whole day, the men stay in their homes while the women wander about doing "men's" jobs and having fun.

We should definitely mention the tradition of "Gamila", during which the heftiest men would carry a wooden model of a camel around the village, which also had an ox or donkey scull painted with bright colours. They would dance around the camel dressed in fancy costumes singing parodies especially of the current affairs.

Significant elements of folklore tradition are also the "Kapsala", meaning the fires burning during the night of Ayios Ioannis celebration, as well as the "Almyrokoulouro", a pretzel unmarried women eat before Lent, in order to dream of a man offering water, which is meant to be the man they will marry.

Feasts – Festivals

In Euboea the habitants always prepared great feasts, in which they would show their good cheer for life, their faith in customs and traditions, their unique hospitality. With the phrase "Peraste stin tavla mas", people invited to their homes whoever was passing by, while great festivals took place at the central squares of the villages, where the young men and women danced dressed with their local ceremonial apparel, the men with costumes from Lamia or Trikala, centres of the men fashion of the time, and the women wearing their luxurious dresses and expensive jewelry.

Even today, there are many festivals performing in Euboea. At Oraeoi, August the 6th,

the day of St.Saviour, the patron saint of the city, is celebrated in a rather magnificent manner. Furthermore, festive events take place on Clean Monday at the harbour of Oraeoi. In Ayia Anna, on the same day, the visitor can enjoy amusing songs with rude content.

There is also the great feast on the day of the Dormition of the Virgin, on the 25th of July. Religious feasts also take place: in Achladi, on the 23rd of August, in Skepasti, on the day of St. Athanasios, on the 2nd of May, in Prokopi on the day of St. Ioannis on the 27th of May. In Metochi, there are two celebratory days, the 20th of May, which is the feast of St. Nikolaos and the 26th of October, the feast of St. Dimitrios.

In Chalkis, probably the most impressive festival is the one that takes place on Clean Monday, when the locals celebrate the "Koulouma" in the old, traditional way, on the Karababa hill. Every year, on the 29th of August, the day of St. John Prodromos, a three-day long trade fair is organized in Amarynthos as well as in Gymnos on the 15th of August.

Apart from the religious festivals, other events include the "Elymnia" from mid-July until the 15th of August in the villages around Limni, the "Messapeia" in the beginning of June in Psachna, the "Agaleia" end of July in Palioura, the "Squid festival" in July in Chiliadou, the "Kyzikeia", 21-23 of August in Nea Artaki, the "Kanareia", end of August in Eretria, "Konistreia", 15-17 of July in Konistres, "Artemisia", 22-25 of August in Ayios Georgios and finally, the Cherry Festival from 29th May-4th June in Metochi where the visitors can enjoy alongside with the locals a very special traditional feast, with folk music and dance and, of course, plenty of cherries.

Traditional Costumes

The Euboean traditional costumes, which one could occasionally see even until the late fifties, conformed to the traditions of Greece, separated in two categories: the rural and the urban costumes. In Ayia Anna, for example, the brides wore costumes of the rural type, which consisted of two cotton shirts, with long sleeves, trimmed with lace. Over the shirts, they wore the white, embroidered, woollen garment known as "segouna", which gave its name to the whole outfit ("ta kala segounia"). They also wore a red or white apron, with embroidered traditional motifs and a belt with a gilded buckle, the "podolourida". On the head they featured a red scarf on top of which they attached the sheer bridal scarf. On their bosom they had crucifixes and chains as well as the "talara", which were rows of silver coins.

The women in Kymi followed the urban style, which was simple, yet luxurious and expensive. The dress consisted of a white cotton shirt under a silk one, decorated with gold embroidered motifs in the front and the cuffs. The skirt was long, usually made of silk. Finally, a jerkin with flared embroidered sleeves and a yellow cotton headscarf ("tsemberi"), which featured rows of gold coins on the forehead, completed the costume.

Costume from Ayia Anna, Euboea.

Gastronomy

Euboea and Skyros have established a reputation as a small paradise for gourmets. The highly developed fishing industry and agriculture means that the everyday table is full of fresh local produce. Fresh fish and seafood is a specialty in all the sea-side restaurants and tavernas. The local meats and vegetables, cooked in unique combinations, are also highly recommended.

Your gastronomic experience could not be complete without the addition of the excellent Euboean retsina and wines.

The locals usually prefer spicy dishes such as pies with wild edible leaves and small plants, herbs and home-made fyllo pastry, and the piquant peppery cheeses, feta style. The fried bread filled with traditional cheese is delicious, as is the spicy pork sausage with orange gist, hot peppers and lots of oregano, while another specialty, the poached wild goat of Karystos is just mouth-watering.

Finally, don't miss the lobster with spaghetti, a Skyrian dish.

As for desserts, there are the marvelous "soutzoukia" and the traditional baklava of Kymi, as well as the local figs, that are very tasty eaten either fresh or dried.

Classic flavours of the Euboean gastronomy: spinach pie, the traditional salad and the baklawa (dessert made of fylo pastry and walnuts) of Kymi.

Architecture

Euboea is a very interesting island architecture-wise. Although the towns and villages appear to share most of their characteristics from Central Greece, they share many structural elements and forms with the islands of the Saronikos gulf.

The houses in coastal Euboea are built in Neo-classical style, with high ceilings and hipped roofs. Usually, the ground floors are used as shops. Other defining features include long narrow windows, a fanlight over the front door, and ornamentation. The small balconies feature elaborate wrought iron balustrades and the front of the buildings are decorated with designs crafted in plaster. Higher on the mountains, the houses are common, two-storey constructions, where the ground floor is used for storage while the first floor is used as a residence.

1. Venetian castle in Mytikas.
2. The interior of an Euboean traditional house in "Erasmia" Farm.
3. Plaster decoration in the House of the Statues in Chalkis.
4. The Folklore Museum of Kymi.

It is the capital of Euboea prefecture. With a population of over 50,000 it is amongst the ten biggest cities in Greece. It is situated in the middle of the western coast of the island occupying the two banks of the Euripus Strait and it is the gateway to the whole of Euboea. The city (and the island) is linked to the mainland by two bridges, one of which is the major,

THE LADY OF EYRIPUS

cable-stayed bridge that is the trademark of Chalkis, along of course, with the famous tide of Euripus. The city is surrounded by the Euvoikos gulf apart from the south, where is protected by the Mt Vathrovouni and small limestone hills.

Panoramic view of Chalkis.

History

There are two theories about the etymology of the word "Chalkis". The most popular one suggests that it's derived from the Greek "chalkos" (copper, bronze), due to the numerous mines and bronze workshops that used to be all around this area. According to the second theory, the name derived from the Phoenician word "kalchis" meaning laver, because the area was rich in the type of conch used to extract the famous dye from. Greek mythology also mentions the daughter of the river deity Asopos, Chalkis. The city has also been called Chalkodontis, Avantis, Alikarna, Stymphalos, and Ypochalkis.

Palaeolithic findings in Ekso Panaghitsa as well as a Neolithic settlement in Ayia Eleousa, indicate that the area has been inhabited since the prehistoric era. Some Early Helladic findings were discovered in Lefkandi and in Manika, where excavations revealed fifty Early Helladic tombs and a city that stretched over hundreds of acres.

The archaeological site of Manika is situated about five kilometres northwest of the modern city and is presumed to be the prehistoric Chalkis. Most of these remains are now underwater due to the rise of the sea level, but Manika appears to have been a prosperous city because of the bronze mines as well as its role as a sea trading interchange.

The first inhabitants of the area were the Avandes, an Ionian tribe that is also mentioned by Homer, in Iliad, for their role in the Trojan War, when they led the Euboean troops, with a force of 40 ships.

Furthermore, it was there, in Aulis and the waters of Euripus that the Greek forces gathered before the Trojan operation and where is also the set for Euripides' tragedy "Iphigenia at Aulis".

Chalkis was one of the greatest city-states of ancient Greece, with its own alphabet and its own currency and monetary system, which was gradually adopted by the whole of Euboea.

The Roman statues hall in the Archaeological Museum of Chalkis.

The coinage certainly helped commerce but it also brought deep social and political upheavals. The crisis was relieved with colonization. Disaffected sections of society, poor farmers and craftsmen, but mainly the courageous traders and seamen who sought new markets and new sources of raw materials, were the first to head to faraway lands.

The colonists first settled on the peninsula, which was later named after its first inhabitants, Chalkidiki. Then, they colonized parts of Italy, Pithikouses Island and Kymi, on mainland Italy. Later, the colonials of Kymi engaged in trade with the Latins who lived further north, making their town the first ever centre of Greek civilization to come in contact with the Romans. From the descendants of the first Chalkidean colonials, the Romans borrowed the worship of Apollo and also the Chalkidean script, constituting thus, the basis of the Latin and all the Latin-based scripts. Pausanias reports that, along with the Chalkideans, colonials from the ancient town Graea (on the site of modern Tanagra, near

Oropos) travelled to Italy and it is possible that the word Graeci (Greeks) that the Romans introduced at a later time, derived from the word Graeans (citizens of Graea). Other Chalkidean colonies in Southern Italy and Sicily include the towns Imera, Reghio and Zagli but there were many more all around the Mediterranean and all the way to the Eastern coast.

After the end of the "Lelantine War" which, basically, was the dispute between Chalkis and the second strongest city of Euboea, Eretria, over the fertile Lelandion Paedion (plain), followed a rather troubled period during which, Chalkis was by the Athenians who divided their land between 5,000 cleruchs. After the Persian Wars, the whole of Euboea became subject to Athens. Chalkis joined the First Athenian league but it revolted twice. When the Athenians induced most of the Euboean cities to join their new maritime league, Chalkis followed. Later it was incorporated in Macedonia and King Philip mounted guard in Chalkis. That's where Alexander's teacher, the great philosopher Aristotle died.

Chalkis was utterly destroyed by a Roman statesman and general, Lucius Mummius, in his attempt to crush the uprising of the Achaean League against Roman rule in Greece. During the Byzantine period, Emperor Justinian fortified the city in such a manner, that it took the Turks five consecutive attacks to finally take it, in the first Turk-Venetian War in 1470 AD. When the Venetian doge Morozini tried to conquer Chalkis, much later, he found himself in the same position and after four unsuccessful attempts, he was forced to lift siege. Chalkis remained a practically inexpugnable city during the War of Independence because of the fortresses on either side of the Strait. Odysseus Androutsos supported by Psarean ships, tried to take the city by surrounding the fortress from the sea, but after a six-month siege, he retreated and Chalkis remained in the hands of the Turks until the end of the war.

The grave of the writer and poet Giannis Skarimbas, on the hill of Karababa.

After the deliverance, Chalkis started developing rapidly. Unfortunately, by the end of the last century, the renowned wall that surrounded the castle was demolished and the moat covered. During the twentieth century, Chalkis combined industrial and commercial development but mainly tourism and cultural growth in an impressive way. Many scholars and artists have lived there. Among them, the poet, author and dramatist of the 1930's generation, Giannis Skarimbas. His works include Divine Goat (1933), Mariabas (1935), Oulaloum (1936), Figaro's Solo (1938) and the award winning Forward Retreat (1976). His work is characterized by paradoxology, the unexpected and the improbable, a fantasy that can reach the wildest unpredictability and an expressional technique that, in its extreme, can twist and distort the language.

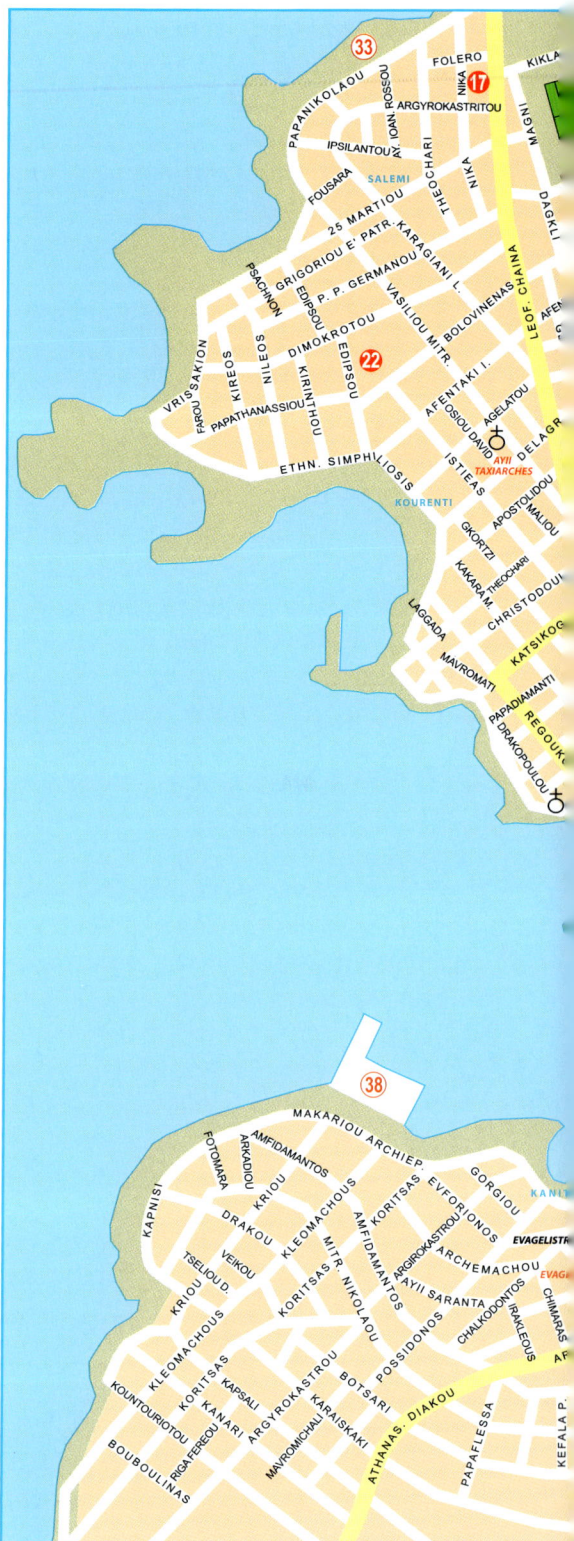

Tour of the town

Chalkis is a buzzing commercial city, with intense tourism and cultural activity and thrilling nightlife. It is a cosmopolitan city that maintains its natural beauty and its close proximity to Athens (81klm) makes it an ideal destination for weekend breaks. The traditional two-storey houses, the bridge and the numerous seaside restaurants and cafes add an air of traditional charm and make it an excellent setting for relaxation and a perfect base for excursions to the rest of Euboea, since the city is situated at the centre of the island. Chalkis, though, is a lot more than a pretty town with lovely slab-paved quarters; it is a modern cultural station with an Archaeological and a Folklore Museum, a library, an art workshop and sporting facilities, a yacht club and many other amenities that cover a wide range of interests and activities and highlights the local history and tradition.

LEGEND

1. Town Hall
2. Prefecture
3. Hospital
4. Police
5. Fire Department
6. Municipal Library
7. Archaeological Museum
8. Court of Law
9. Tax Office
10. National Stadium
11. Municipal Market
12. Municipal Theatre
13. OTE (Hellenic Organisation of Telecommunications)
14. ELTA (Hellenic Post)
15. IKA (Social Security Organisation).
16. OSE (Hellenic Railways Organisation)
17. DEI (Public Power Corporation)
18. KTEL (Hellenic Bus Operators)
19. Cemetery
20. Encampment
21. Playground
22. Prison
23. Fortress

30. Port authorities
31. Nautical club
32. Folklore Museum
33. Tennis court
34. Euripus sound
35. Bridge
36. Vourkou Park
37. Karababa fortress
38. Fish market
39. Tourist Police

VRONTOU
IPIROU THESSALIAS PREVEZIS KIAPEKOU
MIROU CHALKIDIKIS AYIOU IOANNOU KARISTOU GEURGIADI V.
MINIS ERION ERETRIAS AYIOS IOANNIS ALIVERIOU ARETHOUSIS
SYNTAGMATOS MEGALOU ALEXANDROU AEGEONOS AMARINTHION
13 MERARCHIAS EVRITOU PANIONION KATO PANIONIOU AYIOS IOANNIS VOR. IPIROU LORNOU
DIRFON MAKRIDOS 3 MEGASTHENI SYNTAGMATOS AYIOU IOANNOU **19** ERETRIAS
S STRATIOTI CHRIS. SMIRNIS ANAPAPHSEOS KIZIKIOU KATAKOMVIS
AYIA PARASKEVI ASKLIPIADON DIOKLEOUS AMARINTHIOU KRATAIMEANEOUS ACHEOU **4**
ILIVRIAS KONFOLEOS MESSARIOU LILANTION MATOUKA MAVROGENOUS M. RIGIOU
MAGNISIAS PROASTIOU LILANTION ELOPOS PANDOROU DRIOPON ORIONOS ALONAKI SKIATHOU IRAS
OU KARAKLEON ANAPAPHSEOS **9** IPOKLEOUS THEOKLEOUS ARETHOUSIS SKYROU KIMEON ANTIGONOU
LEMPESSI MENEDIATRIDOU DIMITRIOU GAZEPI **19** KOURITON DRIOPON VOR. IPIROU ASOPOU FILON
VOUDIKLARI APOSTOLI KAKARAN TZAVELA ELOPOS PILIKA I. KOURITON 28 OKTOVRIOU ICHALIAS FILOXENOU PALEODIMOPOULOU
NEOFITOU VOKOU KOUMELA AMAZONON **3** IONON KIPROU SAMOU OCHIS ALKMEONOS
PLATOMA MANADIMOU LIKARIOU LENARCHOU IPOVATON ORIONOS EVIAS KIMEON
SOUVALA NEOFITOU DOUKA CHARALAMPOUS GAZEPI CHATZOPOULO PANIDOU PETROGIANI KIMEON
KAKARA M. AGELATOU AVANTON KOTOPOULI PSARON BALALAEON EL. VENIZELOU VOULIAGMENI
TOMARA DIONYSSOU VIRONOS AYIOS DIMITRIOS ARETHOUSIS KRIEZOTOU KAPNISI S. EVIAS
STAVROU P. ANTONIOU MITROPOLEOS NEOPTOLEMOU KASTRO KARAGIANNI N. ANTIGONOU
IFIGENIAS **6** SALONIKIOU PAPANASTASIOU **11** EL. VENIZELOU VELISSARIOU STAMOULI SIOKOU PAPAGI NEOS PERIPHERIAKOS **36**
AYIOS NIKOLAOS ERMOU SQ. AGORAS **7** **13** **18** PHAVIEROU PAPASKIADA **20**
IROON KARIDA KRIEZOTOU SYGROU IOANIDI FILONOS **39** **5** **12** SAVA PAPA G.
FARMAKIDOU **1** **14** KARAMOURTZOUNI **8** FAVIEROU **15** KOTSOU FRYZI TZVIARA **32**
GOVIOU AG. **2** VASILIOU ISSAIOU ANDROUTSOU CHARONDA SKALKOTA
VOUDOURI VARATASI IOUSTINIANOU VAKI MAVROMICHALI EROTOKRITOU AYIA PARASKEVI AYIOS FANOURIOS
TRAPEZOUNTIOU KRITZALI SQ. TZAMIOU MARGARITI STAMATI
KALIA S. PAPALOKA PAVLOU LIASKA PAPASTRATI
KALOGEROPOULOU PEDON
SQ. ATHANASIOU **34**
35
MAKARIOU ARCHIEP. ASTERIA **30**
KARONI PIRROS SKARIMPA THIVON
DELIGIANNI K. KRATIROS DIMITRIOS EVRIPIDOU ATHINON
KALMA IFESTOU IFESTOU **16**
KOLAOU MITR. DELIGIANNI K. **37** PROFITIS ILIAS

OXILITHOU AYIA MARINA LIKOU KIMIS AYIAS MARINAS KIMISOU MARMARIOU
MERGOU PANTAZI X. LIKIDI ALEXIOU
DRAKOMERIOU CHOURMOUZIADOU
VERGI KRIEZON EFPOLIDOS LEOPHOROS
LEOFOROS AVLIDOS NTOURMA LIVARA GEORGIADI THEM. PITHEOS LEOPHOROS AVL.
AYIOS MARKOS GEORGIADI TH. AYIA MARINA PETROT
EVIAS GEORGIADI TH. AYIOU MARKOU OKTONIAS
DMI. POLIORKITOU KARISTIOU EVIAS

AYIOS IOANNIS
19

39

Our tour can begin from the coast of Viotia and the village Kanithos, on the site of the ancient city Kanithos, according to some historians. There, on top of a hill called Phourca, lies the **Castle of Karababa**. The Turks built it in 1864 to protect Chalkis from the Venetians and it was named after the Ottoman general who was buried there, but its Italian design by the Venetian Gerolimo Galopo adds a Venetian rather than a Turkish style to its architecture. Its strategic locality allowed complete control of the Euripus sound and the city of Chalkis. The eastern orientation of the most complex, hexagonal rampart, facing Chalkis, is indicative of the great importance of the fortress for the defence of the city. Two Russian canons of the 19th century are seen on the battlements. The only gate of the castle is on the SE side of the wall. Buildings of military function were built around the gate. A seven-sided tower occupies the west end of the enceinte and is the most substantial of the defensive structures of the fortress and the most impressive one today. Within the perimeter of the walls is a church dedicated to Prophetes Elias, dated from 1895. Outside the walls lies the grave of the great Chalkidean poet and writer Giannis Skarimbas.

1. The church of Profitis Ilias into the Castle.
2. The Castle of Karababa.

From the Castle of Karababa we descend towards Chalkis, crossing the old wooden bridge that is the trademark of the city. It was originally built in 510 A.D., by the Byzantine emperor Justinian. During Turkish occupation the bridge was wooden and stable. In 1858 was changed to a wooden movable one and in 1896 an iron rotary bridge was constructed, that stayed in use till 1962, when the present drawbridge was made. It is a fine observation point to watch the channel tide. Many legends exist, trying to justify the almost unique tide phenomenon. The water-flow in Evripos channel is changing direction about every 6 hours, and sometimes the current can reach the speed of 15km (9 miles) per hour. The phenomenon is probably caused by the strong tidal current of the eastern Mediterranean Sea, which is divided into two separate currents when it reaches the coast of Euboea. One flows into the South Euvoikos gulf, while the other, travelling along the coast, reaches the North Euvoikos gulf with some considerable delay. The phenomenon is intensified by the magnetic pull of the moon and the difference in the sea level between the north and the south gulfs can be easily seen with a naked eye.

The new suspension bridge is the new entrance to the city. Its construction finished in 1993. Being an impressive achievement and built to the south of the old bridge, it consists one of the longest bridges in Europe and it contributes to the easier approach of the city and the relief of the traffic.

1. The old wooden bridge, the trademark of the town.
2. The contemporary suspension bridge.

Along the slab-paved seafront the visitor can see a line of neoclassical buildings of the 19th century, many of which have been restored to their former glory. A typical example of this part of the city is the **"Red House"**. It used to be the residence of the Mallios family and it ornates the Northern part of the city seaside. It was built by the French architect Flegis in 1884. Today it is prepared to function as the "House of Sciences and Knowledge" of Chalkis municipality. The **"House with the Statues"** the lies nearby, took its name from the sculptures that decorate its façade.

Another important building at the seafront of Chalkis is the Kotsikas Mansion, which houses the **Town Hall**. A third building that was the home of the Krieziotis family, houses, today, the **Historic Archive** of the city. Kostou Street, leads from the old bridge to the old Turkish **mosque Emir Zathe** which, up until 1999, when it suffered damage due to an earthquake, used to house a collection of Byzantine and meta-Byzantine sculptures, mosaics and ceramics, Venetian coats of arms etc. It is the only mosque of the eleven in total that used to be in Chalkis and is dated from the first years of the Turkish occupation. There is a small marble drinking fountain near the mosque that features an embossed inscription.

Not a long way from there, is the **church of Ayia Paraskevi**, who is the patron saint of the city. It is a three-aisle basilica with wooden roof that was originally built in the 5th or the 8th century, on the ruins of an ancient temple dedicated to Artemis, Apollo and Leto. It was rebuilt in the 14th century by the Venetians who also added the bell tower. During the Turkish occupation it was converted into a mosque.

In the northeast of the city, at the region **"Kamares"**, is the old Roman Aqueduct that supplied Chalkis with water from "Kambia".

The town's **Folklore Museum** was founded in the early eighties and houses authentic traditional costumes from all over Euboea, hand-

woven textiles, embroideries, weapons, coins etc. There are also two rooms, miniatures of a middle-class house interior with its household articles and a country house with numerous everyday objects and tools. There is also a **Picture Gallery** and **Public Library** where there is a large collection of swords on display, as well as works of the Chalkidean engraver G. Oikonomidis (1891-1958).

Of interest is also the region of Ayios Stefanos. It is believed to have been place of worship of Niriis Arethousa, a deity associated with water and there is a spring with the same name that is believed to have been dedicated to her. Not far from there, a death chamber of the Macedonian style was discovered in the basement of a private home.

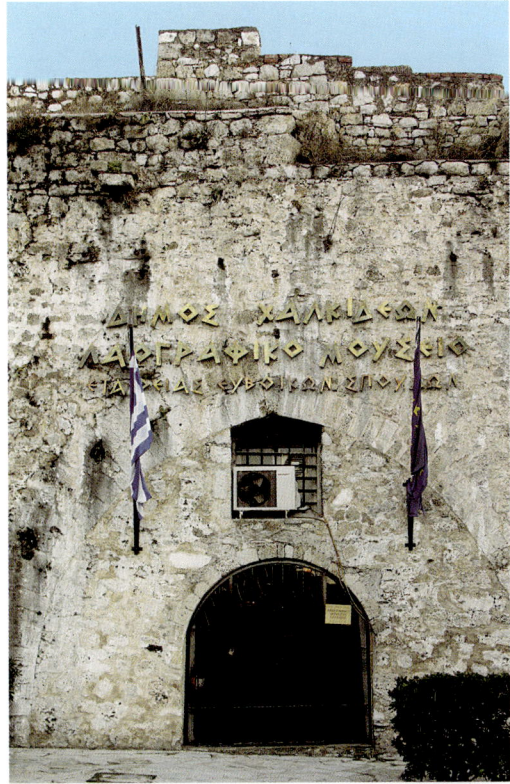

1. The House with the Statues.
2. The Kotsikas Mansion, which houses the Town Hall.
3. The Early-Christian church of Ayia Paraskevi.
4. The Folklore Museum.
5. The mosque Emir Zathe.

The **Railway Station** of Chalkis is one of the most picturesque buildings in the city. It is situated near the old bridge, at the seafront. It was built in 1904 (the year when the first train came to Chalkis) and it features all the typical characteristics of the early 20th century architecture.

There are plenty of wonderful beaches in and around Chalkis that every summer flood with tourists. There is Asteria beach, after the bridge, "Liani Ammos", Souvala, Panaghitsa and Kouredi. A few kilometres away we can find the vast beach of Loukisia (15klm), Alykes and Ayios Minas. They are all ideal for swimming, fishing, eating and clubbing from the morning until late at night.

1. *Forefront of a contemporary church in Chalkis.*
2. *The stone church of Ayia Varvara, which has been discovered during the demolition of the area's walls, in 1897.*
3. *Part of the town of Chalkis, with the Railway Station, at the outskirts of the Euvoikos gulf.*

The **Archaeological Museum**, in Venizelou Street, was built in the early twentieth century and is housing many an interesting findings, covering a wide range of periods. The exhibits include Early Helladic findings from Manika as well as from other regions of the island, mainly Eretria (part of the pediment of the Temple of "Daphnephoros Apollo" (bay leaf bearer), 5th century B.C. Also, Mycenaean pottery and figurines, bronze figurines, Hellenistic and Roman dedicative inscriptions, sepulchral memorials and testimonials.

5

4. Marble horse statue of the Hellenistic period, from the location Treis Kamares, in Chalkis (Archaeological Museum of Chalkis).
5. Relief funerary stele from Nea Lampsakos (Archaeological Museum of Chalkis).
6. A hall of the Archaeological Museum of Chalkis, with statues and funerary steles.

6

5

TOUR OF THE ISLAND

1st ROUTE

Chalkis - Drosia - Anthidona -
Vathi - Aulis (pages 48-51)

ANTHIDONA
Alykes   Agios
Panagia   Minas
Ktonia   Drosia
Loukisia
Agios   AVLIDA   Chalkida
Georgios
Tropaeoforps Vathy   Faros
                      Paralia
                      Avlidas

2h ROUTE

Chalkis - Lefkandi - Vasiliko - Eretria -
Amarynthos - Aliveri (pages 52-65)

                              Seta
                                   Tharounia
                                   Trachili
Chalkida   M. Ayiou
           Georgiou Arna   M. Ayiou
      Mytikas Fylla   Nikolaou Ayios Ioannis
Nea Lampsakos Vasiliko Gymno Ano   Ayios Loukas
      Ayios   Lefkanti Eretria Vathia Aliveri
Nikolaos XIROPOLIS   Amarynthos   Aliveriou
                        Amarynthou

3h ROUTE

Lepoura - Dystos - Nea Styra - Marmari -
Karystos (pages 66-77)

Aliveri Lepoura   Ayii Apostoli
         Krieza   Ayii Apostoli
Dystos   (Petrion)
   DYSTOS   B. Zarakon
Argyro   Zarakes
Almyropotamos
        Mesochoria
        Polypotamos
AEGILEO Nea Styra   Kava Ntoro
IS. STYRA Styra Aktaeo Giannitsi
                        Prinia
                    Kalianos Amygdalia
                    Ayios
Marmari   Dimitrios Kapsouri
   IS. PETALI   Grampia
Megalonisos Karystos
Petalion

4h ROUTE

Lepoura - Avlonari - Oxylithos - Kymi
(pages 78-83)

Kalimeriani Kymi
Pyrgos   Platana
Konistres Oxylithos
Ayios Vlasios Moni Mantzari
        Orio Ochonia
Orologioo Pyrgi Moni Lefkon
        Avlonari
        Achladeri
   Sykies
        Moni Agiou
Lepoura   Ioanni Kranon

Euboea, one of the most beautiful Aegean islands is offered for unique tours; the succession of landscapes, the virgin forests, the magnificent beaches will satisfy even the most demanding visitor. Next, you'll find eight suggested routes, which we consider ideal for a complete picture of the island.

5H ROUTE
Skyros (pages 84-88)

Kyra Panagia
Magazia
Skyros
Aspous
Achill
Peykos
Acherountes
Linaria
Kalamitsa
Tris
Mpoukes

6H ROUTE
Nea Artaki - Dirfy - Chiliadou - Psachna - Politika - Prokopi - Mantoudi (pages 89-95)

Strofylia
Kirinthos
Mantoudi
Metochi
Pili
Spathari
Sarakiniko
Prokopi
Vlachia
Dafnoussa
Ayia Sofia
Limionas
Stavros
B. Chiliadou
Kyparissi
Atali
Agios
Kamaritsa
Makrymalli
Athanasios
Stropones
Nerotrivia
Triada
M. Erioti
M. Panagias Peribleptou
Psachna
Steni Dirfyos
Politika
Katheni
Kastella
Vouni
Nea Artaki
Pisonas
Chalkida

7H ROUTE
Ayia Anna - Vasilika - Artemision - Istiaea - Oraei (pages 96-103)

Artemisio
Agriovotano
Pefki
Ayios Nikolaos
Kanatadika
Asmini
Gouves
Ellinika
Vasilikon
Istiaea
Galatsona
Vasilika
Neos Pyrgos
Orei
Avgaria
Milies
Papades
Ayios Georgios
Monokarya
Fragkaki
Kamaria
Kerasia
Achladi
Agkali
Ayia Anna
Ayia Anna

8H ROUTE
Aedipsos - Lichada - Rovies - Limni (pages 104-111)

Agiokampos
Ayios
M. Ayiou
Aedipsos
Georgiou
Ilion
Gialtra
Ay. Nikolaos
M. Osiou David
Lichada
Polylofo
Drymonas
Ayios
Gregolimano
Ilia
Georgios
Rovies
Retsinolakos
Chronia
Giannitsa
Limni

1ST ROUTE

Chalkis – Drosia – Anthidona – Vathi – Aulis

This first route allows us to visit the beaches that are near Chalkis, on the coast of Viotia. The Municipality of Anthidona occupies the site of the ancient city Chalea. In the heart of Anthidona lies **Drosia**, a small town built among olive groves and citrus fruits orchards that is best known for the surrounding beaches. The first one we come across is **Ayios Minas** that is named after a small church. It is a favourite destination, full of life, with excellent facilities. A little further to the north is the very well known beach of **Alykes** or **Alyki**. It is a long, sandy beach that attracts mainly young people, not just because of the beautiful sea but also because of the lively nightlife. West of Alyki is another beach with crystal-clean water, called **Panayia** or **Panaghitsa**, again named after the small church that lies there. The emerald-green islet opposite Panayia, is Ayios Nikolaos, also known as **Ktyponisi** or **Eglezonisi**. Some water reservoirs and remains of other 7th century structures have been discovered on the island. The nearby Cronia is a picturesque seaside village, where, in the ancient years, used to be a temple dedicated to god Cronus in honour of whom, regular festivities took place, known as Cronia. Not far from there, approaching the north Euboean Sea, is situated the ancient town of **Anthidona**.

It is believed to have been a Phoenician mart, since the area was rich with the special conches from which they extracted the valuable purple dye (kalche). A sanctuary and a temple dedicated to Demeter and Persephone dominated the centre of the town. Anthidona flourished during the Mycenaean era, but was later utterly destroyed by Syllas.

Between modern Anthidona and Mt. Messapio (or Ktypas), lies the **Loukissia** village. It is built on the site of ancient Anthidona and one can see remains of the city walls all over the village, and especially at the seafront. There is also an 800 years old church, Ayios Georgios Tropaeophoros (trophy-bearer). It is a small Byzantine church with a slightly peculiar architecture that was probably built over some convent ruins. Opposite Chtyponisi, at the foot of Mt Chtypa we can see the Mound of Salganeas, a small hill where Salganeas the Viotean is supposed to have been killed by the Persians in 480 B.C., because they thought he had led their fleet into a trap since they could not see the passage of Euripus.

1. The islet of Ayios Nikolaos, also called "Eglezonisi" (English islet).
2. The beach of Panaghitsa.
3. The beach of Ayios Minas, harbour of Drosia.

The small town of **Vathy** is built at the site of the historic Aulis. Despite of it being rather rocky, this port used to be one of the safest in the Aegean Sea, that's why the Greeks chose it as the starting point for their expedition to Troy. According to the myth, Artemis was angry because Agamemnon, the leader of the Greeks, had killed her sacred deer, so she wouldn't allow the ships to sail, unless he sacrificed his own daughter, Iphigenia. The young girl was deceived into believing that she would wed Achilles and was led to the altar. When she realized she had been lied to, though, she bravely offered herself for sacrifice so that Artemis would be propitiated. The goddess, moved by Iphigenia's gesture, she put a deer in her place on the altar and let loose of the winds so that the Greek ships would sail to Troy.

On the **archaeological site of Aulis** there are remains of the temple of Artemis, while the most significant of the findings are exhibited in the Museum of Thebes. In the same museum, one can admire findings from the ancient town Mycalissos, near modern Rizzona. There are many churches and monasteries in Vathy, as well as taverns, cafes and clubs. The road to Athens passes through the village Pantichi, built in the 1920's by refugees from Constantinople. To the south, there are the seaside villages of Pharos and Paralia Avlidas. These are practically an extension of the coasts of Attica and today they are popular resorts. This is also where the shipyards of Chalkis were, of which only one remains.

Views of ancient Aulis.

Roman fresco, depicting the sacrifice of Iphigeneia in Aulis.

2ND ROUTE

Chalkis – Lefkandi – Vasilika – Eretria – Amarynthos – Aliveri

1. View of the beach at Lefkandi.
2. a. Centaur clay figurine of the Early Geometric period
   (10th century B.C., Archaeological Museum of Eretria).
   b. Clay figurine-toy of the Geometric period
   (8th century B.C., Archaeological Museum of Eretria).
3. The twin Venetian towers in Mytikas.

South of Chalkis, in a small distance are the first fishing villages.

Nea Lampsakos was founded by refugees from the city Lampsakos on the banks of Ellispondos, after the population exchange in 1924. Today is a mainly industrial town also known for its fish taverns that offer fresh, tasty seafood. A little further south, opposite Aulis, there is a town with plenty of vineyards and fish taverns.

The road that runs along the coast leads to **Lefkandi,** which is the favourite holiday resort of the Chalkideans. This is the ancient Lelandion Paedion, one of the richest, most fertile plains in all of Euboea and was the reason for the Lelandean War between the two most important cities of ancient Euboea, Chalkis and Eretria. According to Thoukididis, the war lasted a hundred years and all the Greeks took part; making it the first civil war in the history of Greece. The Lelandean plain, which was rich in argil, has been inhabited since the Neolithic period.

During the Early Helladic era, the town of Ksiropolis or Lefkadi appears to have been highly evolved as there were discovered several pottery items and objects from Eastern Mediterranean regions. Even today, the town owes its growth to the river Lelandas

or Vasilico, which provides the fertile plain with much needed water.

Several findings of great importance have been discovered in the vicinity of the **ancient town Lefkadi**. Among them, an arched structure, 47m long and 17m wide, at the centre of which a double tomb was found. Inside there were the very well preserved remains of a woman as well as the ashes of a male, both of noble origin. It is quite possible that the woman was sacrificed after her husband's death and was buried by his side. The man's ashes were wrapped in a piece of authentic woven linen, which, because of the conditions inside the grave, is perfectly preserved. It is an invaluable finding, as it is one of the just two pieces of ancient fabric discovered in Greece (the other one was found in Vergina). In a separate chamber, the skeletons of four horses and a chariot were discovered.

Lefkadi is today a pretty, flourishing fishing village with a wide variety of facilities for the tourists. A little further inland lays Vasiliko, a large town with the river Lelandas or Vasilikos flowing through it. There is a Venetian castle right at the centre of the town that was used to protect the villagers from invasions. The entrance to the castle stands high above the ground to allow for extra protection. The whole structure is in a very good condition.

Vasiliko is a very popular destination for the people of Euboea because not only is it picturesque and charming, it also has all the modern amenities.

One of the prettiest districts of Vasiliko, **Mytikas**, took its name from the goddess Myti, wife of Zeus. She was the patron goddess of the town and there was a sanctuary dedicated to her. The most impressive buildings in Mytikas are the twin Venetian Towers that are visible from the whole of the plain. The towers were mainly defensive structures but one of them appears to have doubled as a dwelling of a local Venetian notable who was in charge of the irrigation of the fields.

Right next to Mytikas is the historic town **Fylla** with its legendary castle. The Italian knight Likarios stormed the fort some time towards the end of the 13th century, following orders from the Byzantine emperor Michael Palaeologos. Likarios had fallen in love with Feliza, sister of Baron Carceri, but was denied her hand, so he vengefully placed himself at the emperor's service. The brave knight indeed managed to storm the castle, captured Carceri and he and his beloved Feliza took up residence in the castle in Fylla. Today the castle is open to visitors.

At the foot of the hill, below the castle, is **Panayia Rizokastelliotissa** or **Rizovouniotissa**. It is a small church, and the rocky slope consists part of its wall. Inside, there are many rare and notable murals and frescos. The great Admiral Andreas Miaoulis' parental home is also situated in Fylla, where during the annual Nautical Week that takes place every August, are organized athletic games named "Miaoulea" in honour of the great man.

Eleven kilometres east of Fylla, there is a monastery with the bizarre name **"Ayios Georgios ARMA"**. In fact, the word ARMA represents the year 1141, although, strangely enough, the church (cruciform with a cupola) is a metabyzantine structure built in 1637 with some parts taken from a protochristian church at the same location.

A new convent has been built next to the old one. (Photo of the convent). To the north of Fylla, we find Aphrati and the "Black Cave". This is a cave with dark walls due to the oxide of manganese.

From Vasiliko, we head south, towards Eretria.

1. The Frankish tower in Fylla.
2. Interior view of the Byzantine church of the Ayios Georgios ARMAS.
3. The Ayios Georgios ARMAS convent, one of the most significant monuments of the area.

2

3

Eretria

The area around Eretria has been inhabited since the Neolithic era. There are findings from Magoula and Pezonissi that prove so. Eretrians founded many colonies, mainly in Napoli, Italy, where they founded Pithikouses, as well as in northern Greece and Corfu. After the end of the Lelandean War in the 8th century, Eretria continued to flourish, even though they had lost. The Persian king Dareios destroyed Eretria in 490 B.C. as a penalty for having assisted Militos during the revolution of the Ionian cities. The city joined the Athenian League but they revolted in 412 B.C. and joined forces with Sparta. They became a member of the League two more times and in 338 B.C. they fell into the hands of the Macedonians.

From 304 B.C. (reign of King Demetrios) onwards, Eretria gains some independence. It was ruled by the cynic philosopher Menedimos (295-268 B.C.) who also founded the School of Philosophy of Eretria. The students of the school later joined the Stoics. During the Roman rule, a lot of the city's artworks were transferred to Italy where they remain until today and gradually, Eretria went on decline. In the years of the Greek War of Independence, after the Turks had destroyed the island of Psara, many islanders moved to Eretria, which, for a while, was called "Nea Psara".

The city as we know it today, was designed by Stamatis Kleanthis in 1834. When Greeks from Asia Minor moved there, they gave the city its old name back, in 1960. In the recent years, the ferry line that connects Eretria with Skala Oropou on the mainland, very drastically helped the already rapid growth of the city.

Today, Eretria shows signs of every single phase it went through in the course of its history. On the corner of Amarysias Artemidos and Archaeou Theatrou Streets, one can still see the ruins of a wall dating back to the years of Menedimos. His political rivals had the structure demolished to build, in its place, a Gymnasium with baths that was also destroyed by the Romans who rebuilt it in the Roman style. Parts of the defensive walls of the city can still be seen in several places. An interesting fact is that both the Psareans and the Greeks from Asia Minor planted eucalyptus trees on and around the towers of the forts in order to avoid the Malaria epidemic that had been affecting the city for quite some time. There are still impressive neoclassical buildings, mansions of the 19th century, like the Korahae residence (1930), the Kourkoubeti residence, the mansion Amarysias Artemidos, the houses of the Papacharalambous and Kanari families etc. as well as many little houses that belonged to refugees.

Next to the local market is the ancient agora of Eretria. Of the numerous buildings, only Tholos remains until today. It is a circular structure of the 5th century that was probably used as a symposium hall. Daphniphorou Apollona Street leads to the sanctuary of god Apollo. The temple was originally built in the 8th century but was repeatedly demolished and rebuilt throughout the history of the city. As a result, it combines architectural elements of various eras, such as Ionian style elements from the second reconstruction and Dorian from the third. The decoration of the pediment is displayed in the **Archaeological Museum** of Eretria.

1. Panoramic view of Eretria.
2. Sculptures representing Theseus and Ariadne from the west pediment of the Archaic temple of Apollo Daphnephoros at Eretria (6th century B.C., Archaeological Museum of Eretria).
3. Relief funerary stele of the Hellenistic period (Archaeological Museum of Eretria).
4. The Archaeological site of Eretria.

1

Another place that is worth visiting is the **"House of Mosaics".** This is a one-storey house, probably built in 370 B.C., featuring an atrium, and other formal as well as utility rooms. It is decorated with exquisite mosaics depicting scenes from the Iliad and mythology. The excavation and reconstruction of the house was carried out by the Archaeological School of Sweden that has contributed a lot to the archaeological research of the city.

The most impressive building of Eretria is, without a doubt, the **Ancient Theatre.** It was originally built in the 5th century but after the Persians demolished it it was rebuilt with cheaper materials. It has a capacity of about 6,000 spectators but unfortunately most of its seats have been stolen. It is constructed on an artificial hill and there is a tunnel leading from the stage to the orchestra.. All the area from the Theatre to the Acropolis is full of ancient monuments, the Upper Gymnasium and Demeter, Persephony and Artemidas Olympias' sanctuaries. There are also some Macedonian graves and the remains of an early Christian basilica.

Modern Eretria can offer her visitors all the amenities and it is an ideal holiday destination since it combines natural beauty with an extraordinary past. Pezonissi island (today it is called **"The Island of Dreams"**) is connected to Eretria with a bridge. On it there is a hotel that shares the same name.

The seafront and all the beaches around Eretria are very well organized and attract many tourists. Some of them are Ayios Andreas and beautiful Linovrochi. The suburbs Malakondas and Magoula are fully equipped with exceptional tourist facilities and are two very popular resorts.

1. Marble lion in the Archaeological Museum of Eretria.
2. Mosaic depicting a nereid on a sea horse, from the House of Mosaics.
3. The arched entrance leading to the orchestra of the Ancient Theatre of Eretria.
4. General view of the Ancient Theatre.
5. The Island of Dreams or "Pezonissi", opposite Eretria.

Amarynthos is a town situated nine kilometres from Eretria. It is built at the foot of Mt Olympos (1,1/1m) and is also known by its medieval name, Vatheia. It has a population of about 5000 and it is only thirty kilometres away from Chalkis. It is a modern resort that is visited by thousands of tourists every year. There has been evidence of human presence in the area since the Prehistoric times. Neolithic settlements have been spotted in the villages Palichoria and Gymno. In the Antiquity, Amarynthos belonged to the city-state of Eretria. So, it folloed closely, from a historical point of view, the neighbouring city.

There was also an important temple dedicated to Amarynthia or Amarysia Artemis. Every year musical and athletic events were held in honour of the goddess. She was regarded the patron deity of Amarynthos and Eretria and the people had dedicated the mountains Olympos and Kotylaeo. The stone columns on which the Eretrians' accords were engraved were kept inside the temple. Therefore, during the Lelandean War, the two cities of Eretria and Chalkis deposited into the temple a convention to wage the war of close quarters..

On the hill of **Palaeochora** there are ruins of a settlement that was inhabited without interruption from the Early Helladic era until the Byzantine period. Today there are only two small Byzantine chapels of the 12th century, the Dormition of the Virgin and the Tranfiguration of the Saviur. The modern town is a fantastic resort with many taverns and "ouzeri" and excellent accommodation. Most of the activities take place on the seafront along with the celebrations for Ayios Ioannis' day, who is the patron saint of Amarynthos, on the 29th of August.

The beaches around the town (Stefanias, Alabeika, Palaeochora, Geranou, Ayiou Konstantinou) are perfect for swimming and relaxation.

Amarynthos.

1

2

In the northwest of Amarynthos, at the foot of Mt Kotylaeo is **Ano Vatheia**, a small village that was built at the bottom of a ravine in order to avoid the pirates' attacks. A little further north there is a road that leads to a women's convent with a 16th century church, which was renovated in 1960. Climbing up Mt Olympos one can see charming little villages. There is Gymno, which is famous for the good quality meat and excellent wine as well as the two Byzantine chapels, Ayios Georgios and Zoodochos Pighi or Ayia. Even higher up, there is the village Setta, situated in an exceptionally scenic environment, among fir trees and famous for its produce of excellent quality sausages and meat in general. The village has a small theatre that was created by actor Nikos Papakonstantinou and operates during the summer months.

Seventeen kilometres from Amarynthos is another seaside town, **Aliveri**, known for its lignite mine and the power plant. It is built on hills near the sea and the nearest beach is Karavos. Other pretty beaches nearby include Ayii Apostoli, Petries, Limionas, Stomio, Cheromylos and Liani Ammos. At a small distance from Aliveri is believed to have existed temple dedicated to "Tamynaeos" Apollo; that is why the municipality of Aliveri is called Municipality Tamynaeon.

On top of the hill Mylaki, there are remains of the Venetian castle **Rizocastro** that is the oldest in Euboea. It is rumoured that there is an underground tunnel connecting the castle to a Venetian tower that today lies within the power plant. The vaulted tomb in Katakalou region that is considered to be a miniature of the grave of Agamemnon is also worth visiting. From the Roman era all that remain are the Baths in the vicinity of Karavos. It is also worth seeing the Byzantine church of **Ayia Paraskevi** for the construction of which several ancient sculptures were used. Unfortunately the Turks destroyed almost all the saints' eyes on the murals.

1. The women's convent of Ayios Nikolaos, in Ano Vatheia.
2. Panoramic view of Ano Vatheia, at the foot of Mt Kotylaeo.
3. A church in Aliveri.

During the Turkish occupation, the citizens of Aliveri resisted vigorously and they contributed a lot to the Greek revolution. The lignite quarries have contributed to the economic growth of the city.

Many small villages such as **Tharounia**, built in the ravine of the river Chondros, belong to the Municipality of Aliveri. It was believed that from this point began the road that led to the Underworld (Hades). Inside the cave Skoteini there were discovered remains of prehistoric animals and a number of objects of the 3rd and 4th millennium B.C. as well as two human skeletons of the Neolithic period. Near Tharounia lies the village **Tracheli** that has a Venetian tower built at its highest point. Travelling towards the southeast we come across the villages Milaki and Prasino, two beautiful way stations on our way to the reservation area of the Dystos lake.

An alternative route from Aliveri is to the village Ayios Ioannis with the monastery of Ayios Loukas were St. Loukas stayed before he went to Fokida. The church of the village is also dedicated to St. Loukas and is very old (1014 A.D.).

Lepoura – Dystos – Nea Styra – Marmari – Karystos

This time we begin our journey in Aliveri and Lepoura and we are headed to the south towards South Euboea and Karystos. In Lepoura, we reach a fork in the road and one can travel north towards Kymi or south towards Karystos.

*The road passes through **Krieza** ("black head"), a village with 900 habitants. East of Krieza, there is a picturesque village, Petries built on the Petries bay. The harbour of **Ayioi Apostoloi** or **Petries Beach** is one of the few on the eastern side of Euboea, opening onto the Aegean Sea. This is a fishing ground rich in a type of fish unique in this area.*

*Beyond Krieza lies the village **Dystos**, named after the lake. It is believed that the ancient town of Dystos was first inhabited in the Neolithic age and it has always been an agricultural community. It seems that, in the ancient years, the locals attempted to drain the lake, scared that the swamp would cause a malaria outbreak. It had fresh water and the banks were reedy. To the east it borders cultivated land and today it is contaminated with biocides and fertilisers. It has also been almost completely dry since 1986 due to extensive use of the water for industrial and farming needs. However, it is still a very significant conservation area for many a rare birds some of which are Mikrotsiknias, Porfyrotsiknias, Phidaetos (a kind of eagle), Nychtocoracas (a type of nocturnal raven) and Petroperdika (a type of partridge).*

*Southern of Dystos is **Argyro** village, the hometown of the great warlord of the War of Independence Nikolaos Krieziotis. The road from Krieza that leads to Almyropotamos cuts through Zarakes with its tiny but beautiful beach, Fournaki.*

***Almyropotamos** (salty river) took its name from a little river with strong currents that has* its sources near Almyropotamos bay and has therefore slightly salted waters. Numerous interesting findings have been excavated in Almyropotamos valley, such as fossilized remains of tiny horses, only about 1.30m tall and having three "toes" in each hoof which belong to the fauna of Mt Pikermi. The assumption that Euboea was conjunct to the Central Greece 13 million years ago was made based on these findings. Between Almyropotamos and Styra there are two small villages with lovely beaches, Mesochoria and Polypotamos.*

The conservation area and wild life sanctuary of the lake Dystos.

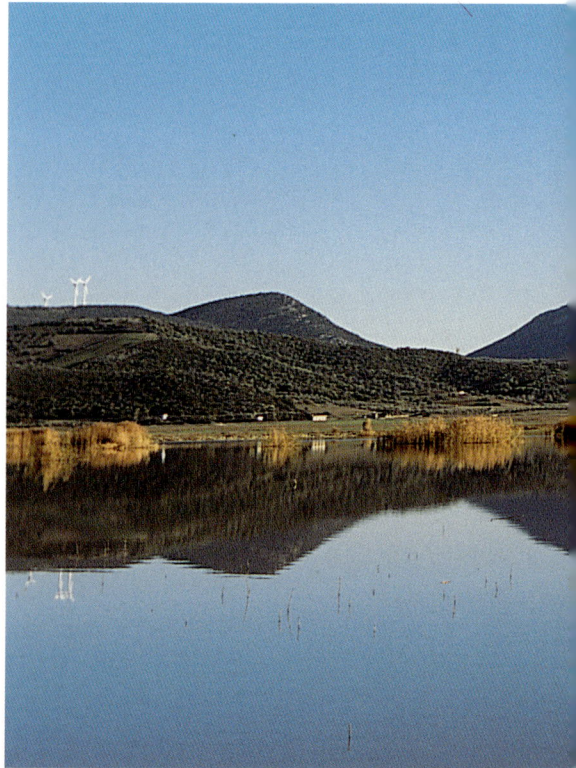

Styra

Styra is an idyllic, traditional village amphitheatrically built in a thickly wooded area in the narrowest point of Euboea so it is closely related to both the Aegean and the Euboean Sea. Again, the area was first inhabited in the Neolithic era and Homer mentioned it in his works. The Dryopes were the first habitants and their main occupation was the extraction and process of the die-producing conches. Styra and the surrounding areas shared a common course of history with the rest of the island until the period of the Frankish rule, when the first Albanian-speaking populations arrived. The second immigration wave came in 1425. These populations were Christianised and blended into the Greek community but their dialect remains until today (Arvanitika).

__Nea Styra__ is a modern resort situated on the shores of the South Euvoikos gulf.

1. Remains of the walls of Styra's Acropolis.
2. Church in Nea Styra.

It is connected by boat with Ayia Marina, on the east coast of Attica. Right at the entrance of the cove that the town is built on, is the islet Styra (the ancient Aegilea), where the Eretrians that were catured by the Persians were transferred there before the battle of Marathonas. There are five more small islands opposite Nea Styra (Ayios Andreas, Fonias, Kondeli, Styra, Petsissi) that are ideal for the keen scuba divers, while many neighbouring beaches like Lefka, Niborio, Kefala, Mesochoria, Tsakei and Porto-Lophia are perfect for swimming.

In the town of Styra itself, worth seeing is the **Castle of Armenon** on top of Ayios Nikolaos hill, with two 18th century churches hidden within the wall. The first one, "Panayia tou Castrou" is built on the ruins of a Byzantine Vasilica. The second one is dedicated to Ayios Nikolaos. In Kokkinomylos, there is a memorial in honour of the hero Petrobeis Mavromichalis and his twelve men who took cover in an old windmill and were tragically killed by Omer-Beis of Karystos. From Nea Styra one can visit the Charakas Gorge, Nimborio, an idyllic beach with a few houses and a little port and also the village Kapsalla, a short distance from Styra.

1. "Drakospito" in Styra, possible used as a sacred ground (ca. 1st century B.C.).
2. General view of the Nea Styra beach.

The most typical sight in Styra and the whole of southwest Euboea though, are the **drakospita ("dragon houses")**. These are massive structures with vaulted roofs, made of big limestone slates. It is not known exactly when or why they were built but we assume they were built some time during the 5th or 4th century and that they were probably used as places of worship. Nineteen such buildings have been discovered with the most impressive one standing high on top of Mt Ochi.

Marmari

Our next stop is the pretty Marmari, on the west coast of Euboea. There are good transport links to Raphena, Attica and that's one of the reasons why this modern resort has become one of the most popular on the island. Marmari owes its name to the coloured marble ("marmaro") that was known since the antiquity, especially in the Roman period, when it was amply used to decorate many mansions. The marble quarries have been found in the area of Kionio and are now open to the public. In Marmari there used to be a sanctuary of Apollo in ancient times.

Off the Marmari coast lies a cluster of small islands called Petalii. They are nine altogether and were created when part of the coast sank.

Views of Marmari, a modern tourist resort, north-west of Karystos.

1

2

They are ideal for scuba diving and fishing and they produce small quantities of olive oil and wheat. According to tradition, this is where the harem of the pasha of Karystos used to spend their winters. There are some fine beaches near Marmari, like Megali Ammos, Fygias, Kokkini and Ayia Irene. Not far away from Marmari, on the east coast of Euboea, is **Ayios Demetrios.** It is a charming little village surrounded by opulent vegetation and crystal clean springs. There is also a little Byzantine church of the 11th century, Ayios Demetrios. The small river that flows through the village falls into a quaint little cove with extraordinary rocky folds. (Photo). Worth visiting is the mountain village Aktaeo from where the visitor can enjoy the breathtaking views of the Aegean Sea and see the Castle of Fylagra. This castle is built at an altitude of 300m and is physically impregnable from the east side.

Legend has it that there is a secret tunnel leading from the castle to the shore. The village Giannitsi has a marvellous deserted beach called Limniona and the village Kallianos up on the mountain with copper, gold and tin deposits. Kallianos is also known for its fantastic sandy 400m long beach that is surrounded by sheer rocks.

Off the Marmari coast lies a cluster of small islands called Petalioi. They are nine altogether and were created when part of the coast sank. (Photo) They are ideal for scuba diving and fishing and they produce small quantities of olive oil and wheat. According to tradition, this is where the harem of the pasha of Karystos used to spend their winters.

1. The beach of Megali Ammos.
2. Aerial view of Marmari.
3. The Ayios Demetrios' village.

3

Karystos

The last stop of our journey is at one of the most beautiful spots on the island, Karystos. It is situated on the coast of the Karystos bay under the imposing Mt Ochi. Karystos is a modern town with a highly developed tourist industry and because of its geographical position it combines the beauties of the mountain as well as the seaside. It was first inhabited in the Neolithic era by the Dryopes but was later colonised by the Avantes. The city took part in the Troyan campaign following the example of other Euboean cities and it was later destroyed by the Persians, led by Datis and Artafernis as a penalty for the town's resistance. During the second Persian war though, the Karystians "εμήδισαν", that is they became the Persians' allies. This had as a result the sack of Karystos by Themistocles and also a fining. Karystos was forced to join the First Athenian League, after the Athenian General Kimon had sieged it.

Karystos was forced to become a member of the first Athenian League, after being besieged by the Athenian general Cimon. The city shared the common fate of the cities of Euboea under the Macedonians and, later, the Romans. The ancient city has been located on the site on which Paleochora now stands. The Romans fully exploited its beautiful, greenish marble. Karystos is also where the story of the brave knight Likarios begins. Likarios conquered the Kokkino Kastro (Red Castle) of Karystos before setting off for the Castle of Fylla on the Lelantios Plain, where he set up base. During the 1821 Greek War of Independence, the successive efforts of the Bishop of Karystos Neofytos, Nikolaos Kriezotis, Elias Mavromichalis and Odysseus Androutsos to liberate Karystos failed. This was also the fate of Nikolaos Kriezotis' siege attempt, which resulted in savage repercussions for the region's unarmed Greek population. Nikolaos Kriezotis ventured a third siege, with the same tragic results.

1. Monument in a square of Karystos.
2. The Monument of the Missing Mariner.
3. The «Kokkino Kastro».
4. Panoramic view of Karystos.

The famous **Kokkino Kastro (Red Castle)**, or **Castel Rosso** (so called because of its wall construction) can be visited and is easily accessible by road. The modern town was built by the Bavarian architect Birbach, an attendant of Otto, the first King of independent Greece and in whose honour the town was named Othonoupolis until 1862, when it took its ancient name once more. Karystos thus acquired an excellent town plan, with wide roads, squares

3

4

and a marvellous waterfront. From the port one can see the Bourtzi, the 15th century Venetian fortress, and the town is brimming with neo-classical houses. The Yiokaleio Foundation houses the fine Karystos **Archaeological Museum**, with inscriptions, sculptures, Ionic capitals and numerous vases, figurines, coins and other noteworthy finds from the area.

The port with the Bourtzi,
the boat-yard and the neo-classical houses in Karystos.

From Kokkino Kastro it is worth exploring **Grambia,** with its strange "double" churches. Unfortunately, one is no longer surviving, having been on the site where the church of Ayia Triada now stands. The other two, those of Ayios Georgios and Ayia Mavra, are joined by a common wall and connected through a door and intermediary wall. Fifty metres before Ayia Triada there is an impressive cave with an underground waterfall, the largest in a Greek cave. The village Platanistos is also interesting, with stunning natural beauty and a wind energy park. South Euboea has many strong winds, an excellent place for setting up wind parks. Many licences have been issued since 1994 for the opening of wind parks in Euboea, the first being that of the Greek Electricity Board and the best known that at Marmara. East of Karystos there are a number of small, picturesque villages, completely untouched by tourism and modern ways of living, truly cut off from the rest of Euboea, thanks to the bad road network. The journey takes several hours, but you can visit Amygdalia, Zaharia, Kapsouri with its livestock rearing and Prinia at Euboea's most easterly point, near Cavo Doro.

1. Interior view of the church of Ayios Nikolaos, the cathedral of Karystos.
2. The Town Hall, in the central square of the town.
3. View of the church of Ayios Nikolaos.
4. The church of Ayia Triada in Grambia, close beside the impressing cave with the underground waterfall.

4TH ROUTE

Lepoura – Avlonari – Oxylithos - Kymi

Route 4 begins at the village of Lepoura, but this time with a northerly direction towards Kymi. From Lepoura the road ascends towards Avlonari. **Avlonari** was built only in the 10th or 11th century by the inhabitants of the surrounding villages that had been destroyed by the Saracenes. The hamlet's "trademark" is the Frankish tower at its highest point. It underwent conservation in 1950 and is one of the best preserved in Euboea. Surviving fortress remains testify that Avlonari was one of the most important local settlements during the Middle Ages. There are the remains of a castle and remnants of wells at the site of Potiri, which appears to have been in communication with other castles of the region. Avlonari has a Folklore Museum, named after Stamatis Chrysostalis, whilst nearby is the Lefka

Monastery, dedicated to Ayios Haralambos, and the church of the Eisodia tis Theotokou, with rare icons and old inscriptions.

Many routes start to the west of Avlonari, leading to beautiful villages, such as **Konistres**, the region's industrial and commercial centre with a weekly trade fair. Ayios Vlassios has a refreshing spring called the Kolethra that gushes from the mountain and irrigates all the surrounding villages. The village of Vrysi has a tragic history, when all its inhabitants were slaughtered by Mohammed II after a siege. Near Kremastos is the Monastery of Klivanos, also known as the Koimisi tis Theotokou. It is not known just when it was founded, but it took its name from its founder, Abbot Klivanios, or Klivanos. The Monastery played a major role in the Greek War of Independence, saving many of the fighters and faithful.

To the east of the central road that leads from Avlonari to Kymi one can visit the villages of **Oktonia** to the north-east and **Achladeri** to the south. Oktonia is only 7 km from Avlonari and is built on a verdant plain above Mourteris Bay, a beautiful beach 70 metres long without any tourism development. From Avlonari there is a road to Pyrgi (2 km) with a 12th-century Byzantine cruciform church, and the martyr village of Orio, where the Abbot Paisios and monk Prokopios were burnt on a spit by Omer Bey of Karystos. There are also lush green Orologi and Ayia Thekla with the 13th-century church of the same name.

From pretty Achladeri one can visit the Monastery of Ayios Ioannis Karyon at Sykies village, with its fine paintings of saints. After the fork in the Alverios–Kymi road towards Orios, we reach **Oxylithos**, the second largest town in the Municipality of Kymi. Oxylithos took its name from the peak (oxy) of the dormant volcano (lithos = stone) at the top of which there now stands a cute little church of the Evangelismos. There are many old churches in

1. The Byzantine church of Ayios Demetrios in Avlonari.
2. The ceiling of a house in Avlonari, richly decorated.
3. General view of Avlonari. At the background, the Frankish castle soars above the town.
4. The beach Achladeri or Achladia.
5. View of the Monastery of Ayios Ioannis Karyon, dated from the 17th century.

this village. On the road for Kymi we encounter in succession Ano Potamia and tourist Platana, from whence commences the road towards Enoria and Taxiarches, where there is a monument to those who fell during the resistance against the Germans. From the site of Fygouli in Enoria, on the road towards Kymi, one can admire a stunning view across the Aegean Sea.

Kymi

Kymi is located approximately in the centre of the island, opposite Chalkis, which is around 90 km away on Euboea's eastern coasts. According to the myth, Kymi took its name from the Amazonian daughter of Poseidon and Lamia. Another version holds that it was so named after the waves (kymata), indicating its nautical history, or from the word "komi" (village). A Mycenean settlement has been found at Kymi, whilst the Kymaians founded colonies in Asia Minor and Italy. Kymi was conquered by Chalkis in the 8th century B.C., subsequently declining. Until the Byzantine period, the city was quite insignificant and exposed to barbarian attacks. The remains of many medieval castles and towers survive in Kymi and the surrounding areas (at Avlonari, Vrysi, Kalemerianous, Oktonia, Kadi, Kipous, Koili, Ano Kouroni and Pyrgi). The area was completely abandoned during the Ottoman period. The first builder of the new Kymi was the livestock farmer Velissarakis in 1668, who secured a settlement licence from the local Turkish Pasha. Others followed suit, and Kymi was thus founded anew. Thanks to its location, Kymi participated to the fullest in the struggle for Greek independence, contributing 45 ships. The population began to increase constantly after independence, whilst direct access to the Aegean Sea gave it shipping and commercial potentials. The first Merchant Shippers' School was founded in Kymi by Papageorgis Oikonomou. Kymi was also the hometown of the internationally renowned medical doctor and inventor of the Pap Test Georgios Papanikolaou.

1. The cathedral church of Ayios Athanasios.
2. The "Mantzari" Monastery, built in the 11th century.
3. Panoramic view of Kymi.

Today's town is built spread out within a lush green surrounding, two hundred feet above sea level. With a magical view over the sea, it has justly been called the "balcony of the Aegean". There are many neo-classical houses and the town is adorned with numerous mansions and beautiful churches. The waterfront is the centre of commercial and tourism activity. Here you can enjoy local products, such as dried figs, and buy the celebrated "koumiotika" silks. Inside the town the **Folklore Museum** is definitely worth a visit, with traditional costumes from Kymi, household objects, ecclesiastical vessels and vestments, jewellery, etc. You should also visit the church of the **Panayia Laoutsanissa**, with its marvellous icon stand made from Skyrian marble and crafted by Ioannis Halepas, father of Yiannoulis Halepas.

On the road for the town hospital we encounter the church of the Prophet Elias on a hill, with a wonderful view and statue of Ioannis Velissarios, hero of the Balkan Wars, who was a Kymaean. It is worth taking a trip as far as

1,2. Exterior and interior views of the Folklore Museum of Kymi.
3. The port of Kymi.
4,5. Views of Choneftiko, with its medicinal springs.

the **Monastery of the Transfiguration of the Saviour** (5 km), built 250 m above sea level and with a magical view over the Aegean towards Skyros. It may have been built by monks from Mt Athos and acted as a refuge for many persecuted Greeks during the Ottoman period. The Monastery was destroyed by Omer Bey in 1822. You should also go as far as lush green Honeftiko, with its medicinal springs. At Kymi you can enjoy a swim at Soutsini and Platana, which has a pebbly beach. The beach of Oxylithos has never-ending sands, and the River Makiniatis discharges here. You can also take a trip to magical Hiliados. From Kymi, moreover, there is a boat for beautiful Skyros, which is our next destination.

From Kymi we can take short trips to the mountain villages of Meletianous, Kalimerianous (only 3 km from Kymi), Pyrgos, where the house of the Turkish Pasha has survived, and to Andronianous, very close to the Kastrovala fir tree forest. A Mycenean tomb with valuable grave goods has been found at Andronianous.

Skyros

Skyros is the largest and most southerly of the Sporades islands, with an area of 210 square kilometres and lying 22 nautical miles to the north-east of Kymi. There are boat connections to Euboea via Kymi and flights to Athens. The island has a similar shape to that of Euboea. In the north it is lush with pine and cedar trees whilst the south is dry and rocky.

Skyros has been inhabited since Neolithic age, as archaeological finds from around the castle area demonstrate. The earliest inhabitants of the island were the Carians, Pelasgians and Dolopes. As Greek mythology tells us, Skyros was the island that Thetis, Achilles' mother, sent her son to in order to save him from the prophecy that he would be killed if he took part in the Trojan War. Achilles thus grew up in the court of King Lykomedes, dressed as a girl along with the King's daughters. He later had a son, Neoptolemos, with one of the princesses, Deidameia. When Calchas prophesied that without Achilles the Greeks would never defeat Troy, the wily Odysseus came to Skyros and, using his cunning, managed to convince Achilles to follow him. Odysseus returned to Skyros after Achilles' death, this time seeking Neoptolemos, since, according to Elenos' prophecy the son of Achilles also had to fight beneath the walls of Troy. Mythology also has it that Theseus, the king of Athens, also died on Skyros, being thrown from the rocky cliffs by King Lykomedes, who feared for his throne.

During the first Athenian League Cimon sought to expel the Dolopes from Skyros as they were engaging in piracy and were a threat to the free movement of commercial ships towards the north-east Aegean. The Athenian League was then in its early stages and there was a need to accord its political leaders divine approval. Cimon thus transferred the bones of the hero Theseus from Skyros to Athens, and placed them in the Theseion temple. Skyros shared the fate of the cities of Euboea and passed to the hands of the Macedonians and, later, to the Romans. The island flourished during the Byzantine period and became an Episcopal diocese. After the conquest of Constantinople by the Crusaders (1204) Skyros came into the possession of the Venetians. After the raids of the notorious pirate Khayrad'din Barbarossa, Skyros passed to the Turks, then back to the Venetians for a few years, for Turkish supremacy to be established shortly afterwards. Skyros was self-governing during the Ottoman period, without a Turkish garrison on the island. A little before the Greek War of Independence of 1821, however, pursued Arvanites (Christian Albanians) pillaged the island. Skyrians were in the naval crews of Kanaris and Kriziotis during the War of Independence, and the island provided protection for refugees. Along with the other Sporades islands, Skyros gained independence in 1829 and was incorporated into the new Greek state in 1833.

1. The statue of the English poet Robert Brooke, in Eleftherias squre.
2,3.General views of Chora, Skyros.

3

1

2

The island's capital - **Skyros** or **Hora** - is built on the west slope of Mt Olympus in the north-east section. It is the only town or village on the island to lie further than 10 km from the port of Linaria on the west coast opposite Euboea. The spring of Anavalsas, rich in water, irrigates the whole town and the orchards in the valley of the River Kifissos. The valley has been shaped by its waters, which until a few years ago powered the mills of the locals.

The town has a small **Archaeological Museum**, with finds from the wider region, especially Bronze age artefacts from Palamari. The splendid folk arts of Skyros are represented at the impressive Faltaits Folklore Museum. The "Skyrian House" near the Folklore Museum was a gift from the Yialouris family and is a fine example of a traditional Skyrian house.

It is worth climbing up to see the view from the **Kastro**, the Byzantine castle with defences and the ruins of the church of the Panayia (Virgin Mary), built during the reign of the Byzantine emperor Leo the Wise. There is a marble lion built into its entrance. Inside the castle we can also see the church of Ayios Georgios Skyrianos (Saint George the Skyrian), with its rare paintings of saints, built by Ioannis Tsimiskis and Nikephoros Fokas in 906.

Skyros town has typical Aegean island architecture with a strong local colour. The houses are stuck together, one- or two-storied, with external stairs, whilst the narrow alleyways are paved in stone. Externally, the houses are cube-shaped, whitewashed and unadorned, whilst inside by contrast they have a rich wood-carved decoration.

1. Linaria, the port of Skyros.
2. View of Magazia, significant tourist resort of the island.
3. Beach Atsitsa, at the west of Skyros.
4. Typical island alley in Chora.

The Megali Strata (Great Road) cuts through the town, leading to Aeonias Piisis (Eternal Poetry) Square, with its statue of the British poet Rupert Brooke, who died on Skyros during the First World War. Windy alleyways come off from the central Megali Strata, leading to all the corners of the town, with folk art shops, in particular pottery, woodcarvings and embroideries on the famed local silk textiles.

Skyros has many beaches with developed tourism. Below Hora is **Magazia**, one of the island's most beautiful beaches. There is also **Molos**, with the old Skyrian stone quarries nearby to it, and **Pera Kampos** on the same side. On the western side of the island, near Linaria, are **Kalamitsa**, **Acherounes** and **Pefkos**. With a small caique boat we can view the Pentokali and Diastrypti caves, and visit the islet of **Sarakenos**. The tourist resort of **Aspos** is located halfway between Hora and Linaria, overlooking the idyllic cove of Achili, from where Achilles set sail for Troy. The north of the island is also beautiful, with fine beaches at **Ayios Petros** and **Kyra Panayia**. The landscape under the shadow of Mt Kochylas in the south is rocky, although the view from Treis Boukes is magical. This is a natural harbour, the entrance of which is closed off by the islets of Plato and Sarakenos. At Treis Boukes lies the grave of Rupert Brooke, who died here on his return from Gallipoli.

The little Skyrian horses are an island feature. Only a metre or so tall, they are known to us from ancient sculptural reliefs. They roam freely, particularly in the south o f the island, although their population is declining and a systematic effort is therefore being made to save them. Skyros is also known for its Carnival and the custom of "the old man and the girl" that takes place on the final Carnival Sunday. The young men of Skyros wear either black caps with giant bells and pretend to be "old men" or Skyrian bridal gowns and pretend to be the "girls". A procession is formed of the "old men", "girls" and "Franks", and the island's residents gather to await them. The dancers go down the road into the square, with much dancing, singing and shouting.

Nea Artaki – Dirfy – Chiliadou – Psachna – Politika – Prokopi – Mantoudi

Our sixth route starts from Chalkis and goes as far as the island's northern section. First stop is **Nea Artaki**, only 4 km from Chalkis and essentially an extension of it. The earliest archaeological finds in the whole of Greece were uncovered at Nea Artaki – stone tools and hunting equipment around 500,000 years old. Traces of a neolitihic settlement have been uncovered in the wider area. The archaic city of Batondas, a suburb of ancient Chalkis, was located in the vicinity of Nea Artaki. The legendary knight Likarios was active here during the Frankish period. Having taken northern Euboea, he set up an excellent trap at this point and awaited the attack of Guiberd and John de la Roche, duke of Athens, who were defending Chalkis. He beat them and nearly achieved his ultimate goal to take the city. But his plans were undermined by the reinforcements that arrived, and so he withdrew, taking the Castle of Fylla where he based himself. The area was a constant battle zone during the Greek War of Independence. In more recent years, the settlement of Greeks from Asia Minor after 1922 was a great boon to the town's development.

Today it is a modern market town, which borders onto Chalkis. The little church of the Panayia Faneromeni stands out, built in honour of the miraculous appearance of the Virgin. Crowds of faithful gather here on her feast day on 23rd of August.

1. The beautiful beach of Pefko, which is accesible only by a footpath.
2. View of Kato Steni which, along with Ano Steni, consist a place of great tourist resort.

From Nea Artaki the road to the east leads to the mountain massif of **Dirfy**. In ancient times there was a temple of Dirfya Hera on Delfi, the tallest peak of Dirfys (1,743 m), in honour of the weddings of Hera and Zeus that took place here. Another version of events says that Hera's temple was actually on Tanais, the second tallest peak of Dirfys. Almost at the borders with Nea Artaki we encounter **Pissonas**, a village with a population of around 600, a Venetian tower in good condition and Kathenous, on the foothills of Dirfys. Around one and a half km from Kathenous is Eria Monastery, a 13th-century Byzantine church that survives complete. After Vounous we reach **Kato Steni**, which, along with **Ano Steni,** are among the most popular destinations in Euboea.

The name derives from the shepherds who during the Ottoman period would repel Turkish attacks in a narrow ("steni") pass, where today's square lies. During the Ottoman era it was called Kleisoura ("closed") because it was inaccessible and was the hideout of the local bandits and armed warriors. You can even search for the Karaouli of the Stenioton, a large rock that was used as a lookout post over the whole area.

Today it is a very pretty village, with many tavernas celebrated for their good meat and tasty wine, and many springs with clear, refreshing water. You will see little improvised bridges across the gushing streams at many points along the road. At **Stropones** survives a Byzantine church, the Koimisis tis Theotokou (Dormition of the Virgin), whilst at **Theologos** is the Koimisis tis Theotokou Monastery. Inside the church there is a rare icon with both Ayios Georgios and Ayios Demetrios.

From the village of **Ayios Athanasios** one can walk through the beautiful Agali ravine. The ascent up Dirfys affords an exceptionally beautiful route through fir, chestnut, pine and plane trees. There is a shelter and ski centre at the peak of Dirfys. On the other side of Dirfos the road descends to the beautiful sandy **beach of Chiliadou,** with developed tourism and a nudist beach towards the end.

Continuing north from Artaki we reach **Psachna**. The region has been inhabited since Neolithic age, and it appears that the settlements here came under the rule of Chalkis in antiquity. The city was destroyed by the Turks in 1470, whilst today's town was built later by

refugees from Samos. At the entrance to the town is a statue of the Euboean hero of the War of Independence Angelis Govios, who was killed by the Turks. It is worth visiting Makrymallis Monastery, with its very old church, and the Monastery of Ayios Ioannis Kalyvitis about 4 km north-west of Psachna. The church was built in the 13th century and has exceptional wall paintings, whilst there is a dedicatory inscription in the conch. A little outside Psachna is **Kastella**, on the site of the ancient city of Argoura. Some of the most decisive battles of the War of Independence took place here, during one of which the hero Angelis Govios, whose statue we saw at the entrance to Psachna, was killed.

From Psachna we can go down to the beautiful beach of Politika. **Politika** has been inhabited since neolitihic times and is today a village with traditional architecture, stone houses and substantial tourism. One of the best preserved Venetian towers stands in the square, whilst the **Monastery of Panayia Perivleptou** stands on a rise. This has a cruciform church with a dome, built in 1205. Northwest of Psachna (12 km), in among the pine forest, is **Stavros**, a mountain village at an altitude of 350 m, with a fantastic view over the Euvoikos gulf. From Psachna we can also visit **Kamaritsa** and **Nerotrivia**, which took its name from the practise of processing hair by rubbing (trivia) it in the rivers (nero, waters).

1. The beach of Chiliadous, with the wild natural beauty and the huge, during the last years, tourist development.
2,3. Exterion and interior views of the 16th century church of Panayia Perivleptou.

The road from the east of Psachna leads to **Kontodespoti** and to **Triada**, where Admiral Nikolaos Krieziotis lived in a house that still stands.

A little further along is Attali, with the ruins of a 10th-century church, whilst nearby is the plateau of Tanais, of great natural beauty, and the Voidokleftra cave. You can continue the route from Stavros to north Euboea through the village of Kyparissi, for Ayia Sophia, with the beautiful beach of **Limniona**.

Taking a northerly direction from Psachna, we follow the bed of the river Kereas and arrive at **Prokopi**, where the relics of Ayios Ioannis the Russian lie. Most of the population are Asia Minor refugees, who brought their customs and traditions with them, one example of which are the aforementioned relics of Ayios Ioannis the Russian. The refugees from Prokopi in Asia Minor brought the relics of their beloved Saint, who had died and was buried at Prokopi, with them in 1922. The Saint's body remained untouched until it was exhumed, when it was placed in an urn as a religious shrine. His memory is celebrated on 27 May, when crowds of worshippers gather at Prokopi.

1. The relic of Ayios Ioannis Rossos, which is on view in the interior of the church.
2. Exterior view of the church.
3. The impressive carven chancel screen.

The village is lush green, with many plane trees, two of which present the strange phenomenon of twin plane trees – two plane trees joined together. From Prokopi we head east towards **Pili**, which is connected to the Sporades, or follow the beautiful coastal route to **Sarakeniko**, a delightful Aegean beach, and former pirate hideout. At Pili we can marvel at the rare wall paintings in the little Byzantine church of Ayios Ioannis Theologos and swim in its lovely, windless beach.

The road north from Psachna follows the bed of the River Kereas as far as **Mantoudi**. The inhabitants of Mantoudi were slaughtered with axes ("peleki") by Turkish pirates in 1795, and for this reason the region of ancient Kerinthos was named Peleki. Today's Mantoudi is a modern market town popular with tourists thanks to the nearby beach of Kymasi, which is bursting with life in the summer months.

To the west is **Daphnousa**, a pretty verdant village on the foothills of Mt Kantili and with a delightful Venetian tower at a very high point. The route through the wonderful Euboean natural landscape, brimming with trees and gushing waters, is breathtaking.

From Daphnousa we can go towards the pretty **Spathari** and **Metochi** to reach **Kerinthos**, a little further up from Mantoudi. Ancient Kerinthos was one of Euboea's finest cities, and many important archaeological finds have been made here. Today's town, cooled by the waters of the Voudoros River, was settled by refugees from Asia Minor. From Mantoudi and Kerinthos the road passes through the charming village of **Strofylia**, and forks off for Ayia Anna and Limni.

1. Prokopi.
2. The twin plane trees.
3. The beach in Kymasi.
4. Mantoudi.
5. The Nileas river in Prokopi.

Ayia Anna – Vasilika – Artemision – Istiaea – Oraei

Our next stop is Ayia Anna, a pretty village that has kept its character despite its tourism development. Although the region has been inhabited since the Palaeolithic era and stone tools from this period have been found, the village was created relatively recently, by a few families in 1776. Ayia Anna has a Folklore Art Museum, in which we can admire traditional artefacts and costumes of the area. At Ayia Anna a traditional feast is held every Kathara Deftera (Clean Monday of Carnival), with plenty of wine and naughty rhyming couplets. Its beach, **Angali**, is well known for its long sands and clean waters. Remains of the ancient city of Trynchai have been found on its northern edge. In the summer Angali is transformed into a tourist resort. Nature lovers can visit the ravine of Boulovinanas near Palaiovrysi, approximately three kilometres from Ayia Anna.

From Ayia Anna we can go to the delightful mountain village of **Kerasia**. Aside from its natural beauty, this village is known for its Petrified Forest, resulting when the area was covered by volcanic lava millions of years ago. This has preserved specimens of rare animals of that era, fossilised animals of Pikermi-type fauna, which are kept at the Palaeontology and Anthropology Museum of Athens.

On the road from Ayia Anna to Vasilika branches out a road for **Achladi**, decimated by the Ottomans for its participation in the War of Independence. The beach of Frangaki is 1,500 metres long with beautiful sands and celebrated for its underwater fishing. At **Prasidi** there is a monument to the fallen of the village. On the Ayia Anna-Vasilika

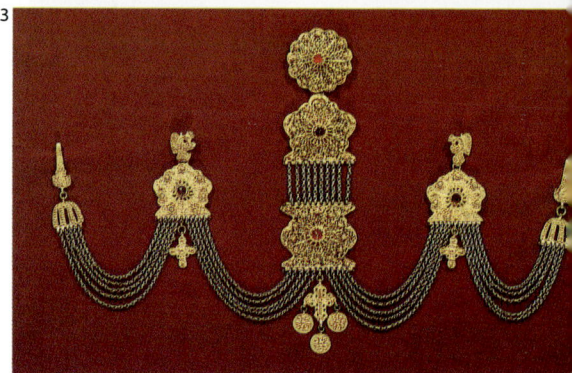

road, through the pine forest, is **Papades**, whilst on the 97th km from Chalkis is the beautiful **Vasilika**, with its renowned Vasilika beach. Today's Vasilika lies at a distance of one and a half km from the beach, but the old site was right on the beach; pirate raids forced the inhabitants to move further inland. Vasilika beach is impressive and has been developed for tourism, as have the surrounding beaches. Near Vasilika we can admire the forest of Tsapournia.

Ellinika is the point at which the Greek fleet anchored during the naval battle of Artemision. The ruins of the ancient fortifications have led to the area being identified with the ancient city of Nyssa. The nearby beach of Ayios Nikolaos is popular with visitors, being very pretty and with a splendid view over the islets of **Myrmingonisia** and **Pontikonisi**.

Agriovotano is built on Cape Artemision, above the road that leads to it, giving a panoramic view of the watery battlefield. Before reaching Artemision town, we encounter **Gouves**, where the poet Georgios Drosinis lived, and whose house still stands today. Near Gouves is the village of **Kastri**, with a wonderful view over the sea.

1. The Folklore Museum of Ayia Anna.
2,3. Pectoral jewellery from the costume of Ayia Anna. They consist of many silver chains.
4. The beach of Ayia Anna.
5. The Drosinis tower in Gouves village.
6. The village Agriovotano.

Artemision

This historic site brings the naval battle between the Greeks and the Persians, which was the beginning of the end for the Persians, immediately to mind. The Greeks had gathered only 270 ships, whereas the Persians had set sail with 1,207! The battle lasted for three days and –thanks to the heroic efforts of the Greeks and the strong winds which threw many of the Persian ships against the coast of Pelion– with a Greek triumph and the decimation of the Persian fleet, which was finished off at the Battle of Salamis. Strong winds really do blow here, and there have been many shipwrecks as a result. Thanks to these, many examples of ancient art have come to the surface, such as the two bronze sculptures found by Sporadian fishermen in 1928. One is the composition of the horse and young rider and the other the sculpture of Poseidon (or Zeus), now on display in the National Archaeological Museum in Athens. The general region of Artemision was dedicated to the goddess Artemis in antiquity, and the remains of her temple have been found on Muscat hill, near the little chapel of Ayios Georgios.

The hamlet of **Pefki**, an extension of Artemision, today has a wonderful organised beach, 2 km long, with wonderful modern tourism and hotel facilities. The distance between Pefki and Kiathos is very close, and private speedboats have easy access. From Pefki we can go to **Gerakios**, with a wonderful view of Pagasitikos gulf. The lovely fishing village of **Asmeni**, near Pefki, is great, with tavernas along its pretty beach.

1. A beach in Artemision.
2. The 2 km long sandy beach of Pefki.
3. View of a house in the fishing village Asmeni.
4. Panoramic view of Artemision.
5. The port of Pefki.

Istiaea

Istiaea is the capital of North Euboea, situated in the centre of a small plain at one of the island's more northerly points. It is 130 km from Chalkis and built a short distance from the beach. The history of Istiaea begins in Neolithic age, as archaeological finds have shown. At Oraei archaeological excavations have also brought to light a settlement and finds dating to the Early, Middle and Late Helladic and Mycenean periods. Homer immortalised Istiaea in his catalogue of Euboean cities that took part in the Trojan war. After the Trojan adventure, Istiaea experienced great growth, as did neighbouring Oraei. Istiaea's fate changed with the naval battle of Artemision, when it was destroyed by Xerxes' troops that were stationed there. It later became a member of the first Athenian League. Pericles punished the city severely after its subsequent withdrawal from the League, exiling all the inhabitants to Thessaly and settling Athenian "cleruchs" (land settlers) there instead. In the later Ottoman period it was part of Ali Pasha of Ioannina's dominion, and was also the place where the War of Independence was declared and the first national liberation battles fought.

Today Istiaea is the largest town of North Euboea, with around 6,000 residents and a particular local colour, thanks to its old stone built houses and neo-classical mansions, a typical example of which is the old Voulgaris residence. The town has a very fine Natural History Museum and all the comforts of modern living. Istiaea sees significant commercial and tourism activity in both winter and summer, being renowned for its local delicacies that are served in the many quaint old tavernas throughout the region.

Views of Istiaea.

Five km to the north of Istiaea is **Kantadika**, a coastal hamlet recently experiencing much growth. There is a wetland in the area, formed by two small lagoons, small and large Livari. Their salty waters are full of reeds and rich in vegetation, amongst which live rare species, such as the Ciconia stork and the little gull. This wetland is a way station for migrating birds, such as the glossy ibis, spoon bills and swans. Istiaea is essentially one urban zone along with the neighbourhoods of Neochori, Ayios Georgios,

Ayios Panteleimonas, Sinasos (founded by refugees from Cappadocia in Asia Minor and built over two hills with a magnificent view) and Panayia Dinious, with its lovely natural environment and homonymous church.

There is a folk collection at Sinasos. From Istiaea we can visit Kamaria and the verdant Vouta, at the foothills of Mt Telethrios. Six km from Istiaea and next to the bed of the river Xeria, the road leads to **Monokarya**, **Milies** and **Kokkinomilia**. Another road leading from Gerakios passes through the villages of **Galatsonas** and **Avgaria**.

At a short distance from Istiaea is the historic site of **Oraei**, the history of which is linked to that of neighbouring Istiaea. The area was inhabited from the neolithic period and there are finds at Neos Pyrgos. Oraei shared the fate of Istiaea when it too left the Athenian League, and passed into Sparta's sphere of influence after the end of the Peloponnesian

War. The Platonic philosopher Euphraios was born here, becoming politically active and attempting, in vain, to curtail Macedonian influence. A Macedonian garrison was finally established in the city, and much later it came under Roman control. The periods of Frankish and Ottoman rule followed, as in the rest of Euboea. Today's town has an excellent layout, planned by a Bavarian architect and the Greek engineer Stamatis Kleanthis. There are a number of little tavernas on the beach, along the length of the port, and this is also the focal point of tourist life, particularly in the summer months.

Near Oraei is **Neos Pyrgos**, a once marshy area that has now undergone impressive tourism development and is today among the most fertile, cultivable terrain in North Euboea. On route from Pyrgos to Aedipsos is the gorgeous beach of Nisiotissa. There is a rocky islet a short distance from dry land upon which survive the remains of a medieval tower. Four km from Oraei is **Taxiarhis**, another village revived by refugees, who made it one of the most cared for and clean villages of Euboea. A dirt road leads to mountain Kastaniotissa, which can also be reached must easier through Istiaea.

1. The bull of Oraei, from a funerary monument of the 4th century B.C., has been discovered in the port of the town, in 1966.
2. The village Pyrgos, one of the most fertile areas of the island.
3. View of the village Milies.

8TH ROUTE

Aedipsos - Lichada - Rovies - Limni

Our eighth and final route covers the western edge of Euboea from Aedipsos and closes the cycle of our tour at Limni. Aedipsos lies around 120 km to the north-west of Chalkis, and has been known since antiquity for its medicinal springs and the therapeutic quality of its water. There is a boat connection with Akritsa in Fthiotida, whilst Ayiokampos is also connected to Glyfa. Aedipsos's historical fate has been connected to its medicinal springs. The therapeutic qualities of its waters were known from antiquity and have been mentioned by many ancient writers. Strabo talks of the springs of Aedipsos as "Herakles baths" and tradition holds that this is where Herakles regained his lost strength. Aedipsos has been inhabited since Neolithic age, whilst in antiquity it came under the sphere of influence of Istiaea. Its history does not differ much from that of the other cities of Euboea, the only difference being that Aedipsos did not play a major role as it had the same character then as it has now: a quiet and lovely spa town.

With the passing of the centuries; the springs underwent many changes. Extreme geological phenomena, such as earthquakes, affected the flow of the waters, creating many new springs. Aedipsos became famous throughout almost the whole world in the Roman period. It was visited by the Roman general Sulla in his effort to cure his "podagra", i.e. the arthritis and rheumatism in his feet from which he suffered gravely. He built baths, the Baths of Sulla, of which only a few ruins survive today.

1,2. The "Thermai Sylla" hotel, one of the sights of Aedipsos.
3. The medicinal springs of Aedipsos are known since the antiquity.
4. Beach in Aedipsos, where visitors enjoy the medicinal baths.
5,6. Views of Aedipsos.

5

6

Aedipsos was also visited by the Roman emperors Augustus, Hadrian, Marcus Aurelius, Septimus Severus and Caracalla, as well as by the Byzantine emperors Constantine the Great and Theodosius the Great. Near the springs are the remains of the ancient city and of the 2nd and 3rd century A.D. bathhouse facilities, which were also used in the Byzantine period. The city was destroyed by the Turks in 1814, whilst commercial use of the springs began in 1887. It was during the inter-war period that Aedipsos truly flourished, with famous visitors from all over the world. There are around 60 springs, with temperatures of 34-71.2 degrees Celsius, making them among the hottest in Europe. The hot waters are due to the great crack in North Euboea.

Today Aedipsos is a modern spa town with developed tourism, hosting around 40,000 visitors daily, and hydrotherapy units. Many of its buildings have been renovated, and it also has luxury hotels, rented rooms, restaurants, tavernas, ouzo restaurants, fish tavernas and steakhouses. At the Greek National Tourism Organisation hydrotherapy units you can see a number of classical archaeological finds on display, whilst the Roman finds are housed in Chalkis. The "Thermai Sulla" hotel, built in 1896 and renovated a few yeas ago, is an impressive building.

At Ayia Paraskevi there is a Venetian tower and a little church dedicated to the Saint. Also near Aedipsos (6 km) is the village of Ayios, with no tourism infrastructure but with the beautiful beach of Ayiokampos. In addition to its ferry-boat connection to Central Greece, Ayiokampos sees much tourism thanks to its beautiful sandy beach.

After the beach of Ayios Nikolaos, the visitor can enjoy the nature and charm of the coastal settlements of Yialtra and Gregolimano. This is the most westerly point of the peninsula, the cape of Lichada. The peninsula has been inhabited since the neoloithic period, and it appears that there was an important city here in the classical era, which lasted until the Romans. Yialtra has medicinal springs, and its history has thus always been identified with that of Aedipsos. It is comprised of two hamlets, the older village and the newer coastal hamlet with its flourishing tourism. Because of the bad road network, the distance between Yialtra and Aedipsos can be more easily and quickly covered by sea rather than by land.

Gregolimano is a large organised beach full of hotels and tourism facilities. The road further west along the edge of the peninsula leads us to the village of Lichadas. Mythology holds that Lichadas took its name from Lichas, the servant of Hercules, whom the demigod flung when he gave him the chiton that had been poisoned by his wife, which he then wore. The mythological version of events says that the islands of **Lichadonisia** mark the point where the body of Lichas fell into the sea. The scientific version says that the Lichadonisia were created as a result of the geological, volcanic phenomena in the submarine zone. Archaeological finds of the 6th and 7th centuries have been found on Strongyla, the largest of these islands. Along with the smaller islands, the Lichadonisia create a wonderful sight.

Lichada and the beach of Ayios Georgios offer the visitor all modern comforts, whilst the northern part of Lichada is still almost unexplored, with virgin nature, and better accessible by boat.

1. *Roman female statue discovered in Aedipsos (1st century B.C., Archaeological Museum of Chalkis).*
2. *The church of Ayia Paraskevi in Aedipsos.*
3. *Panoramic view of Glyfa.*
4. *The village Ayios, with the beautiful beach of Ayiokambos.*

1

2

To the east of Aedipsos is the village of **Polylofo** and the pretty **Elia**. Elia has seen much tourism development in the past few years. A coastal village with a beautiful beach and delicious fish that are served in its many fish taverns. This is where the Monastery of Ayios Georgios Elias is located, built quite high up with a stunning view. To the east the road continues along the coast and towards the fir-filled **Rovies**. This village is also coastal, built in the fork of the mountains Xeros and Telethrios. We have signs of human presence in the area from as early as the Palaeolithic period and throughout all the later Historical periods. The Venetian tower in the centre of the village is a remnant from the Frankish period. Rovies has a wonderful beach, meaning that the village is quite busy, particularly in the summer. From Rovies we can visit the Monastery of Ayia Irene Chrysovalantos in the west, as well as the renowned Monastery of the Blessed David. This was built by the Blessed David himself, circa 1550, on the ruins of an ancient temple.

Within the church, which is dedicated to the Metamorphosis of the Saviour, are preserved the sacred bones of the Blessed David, his incensory and his stole. The Monastery also contains the tomb of the monk and long-time Abbot of the Monastery, the Venerable Iakovos, known for his beneficence. The mountain village of **Drymonas** is very close to the Monastery of the Blessed David, and was built after the Monastery's foundation. Taking the coastal road from Rovies we are led to the beautiful beaches of Chronia and Retsinolakos. They belong administratively to the province of Limni and are inhabited mostly by refugees from Asia Minor and their descendants.

Limni

The beautiful region of **Limni** lies 85 km to the north-west of Chalkis, spreading out over the cape, between Mounts Telethrios and Kantili. We have specimens of human presence from the palaeolothic period, which have been found at Rovies and Ayia Anna, whilst neolithic settlements have been located at Limni and Kerinthos. Limni has been identified with the classical city of Elymnion. Thucydides mentions that a section of the city was sunk by a great tidal wave, which was created by an earthquake. It is also believed that the ancient city of Aeges was located in the vicinity of Galatakis Monastery.

From the 16th century onwards the region witnessed continuous habitation and economic prosperity as a result of the sailing skills of its people. Angelis Govios, hero of the Greek War of Independence, was from Limni. After Independence, the Limnians played a major role in the development of Greek shipping. Limni is the birthplace of the heroes of the national resistance during the Second World War –Lela Karayianni, Kostas Karageorgis and Kostas Gambetas– and also of the caustic chronicler Nikos Tsiforos. Today's Limni preserves its traditional architecture, blended with many island features, with pretty lanes and numerous Byzantine monuments. Characteristic is the little church of the Zoodochos Pigi, inside the town, with its mosaic floor. The town has a Historical and Folklore Museum, which houses an archaeological collection from the area, objects and weapons belonging to Independence fighters, and valuable documents. The Museum of Marine Biochemistry –5 km on the road for Galatakis Monastery– is also worth a trip, with fossilised exhibits from the seabed. Limni is a much loved tourist destination for its beautiful beaches, the modern comforts of its hotels, and its numerous little taverns. Nearby is Kochylis beach, Ayios Georgios and the delightful area of

1. The Ayia Irene Chrysovalantos Monastery.
2. View of Limni from the sea.

Katounia. Limni has a vibrant cultural life, with a number of cultural and sporting associations, and several events are organised throughout the year, the climax being the "Elymnia" festival. We must not forget to visit the Monastery of Ayios Nikolaos "Galatakis", built in the 7th or 8th century over the foundations of an ancient temple to Apollo. The church and chapel are adorned with many beautiful wall paintings, whilst a secret passageway leads from the annexed chapel of Ayios Ioannis Prodromos (St John the Baptist) to a crypt in the roof of the church. The tower on the west side of the Monastery, built in the 15th century, today houses its Library, with Greek and Turkish documents.

With Limni as a starting point, you can attempt to go up to the mountain villages of **Mourtia**, the verdant **Kechries**, with the fountain of Erotokritos, and **Daphne**. You can also visit the mountain village of **Kourkouloi** and **Skepasti**, with its cool waters and springs.

From Kechries the road meets that from Strophylia and continues towards Nea Artaki and Chalkis.

1. The unique beach in Kochyli, near Limni.
2. The beach of Limni.
3. Panoramic view of Limni.

Text: HELENA SPYROPOULOU, NIKOS VASILAKOS
Text editor: DIMITRIS ANANIADIS
Translation: RANIA TSITSIKA
Design: EVI DAMIRI
Layout: RANIA TSILOGIANNOPOULOU
Photographs: M. TOUBIS S.A. ARCHIVE

Colour Separation – Printing: M. TOUBIS S. A.